Job Free

Four Ways To Quit The Rat Race,
Achieve Financial Freedom,
And Live On Your Terms

by Jake Desyllas

Job Free

The Voluntary Life Press

Job Free: Four Ways To Quit The Rat Race, Achieve Financial Freedom, And Live On Your Terms

Jake Desyllas

Copyright © Jake Desyllas, 2015

First Published by The Voluntary Life Press, 2016

Contents

Introduction
1

Chapter One — Extreme Saving
13

Chapter Two — Unjobbing
33

Chapter Three — Lifestyle Businesses
49

Chapter Four — Startups
61

Chapter Five — Choosing a Job-Free Lifestyle
79

Chapter Six — The Psychological Challenge
91

Appendix: About Investing
101

Bibliography
111

Acknowledgements
115

About the Author
117

To P, with gratitude.

Introduction

Whoever will be free must make himself free.
—Max Stirner

Peter's Story

Sometimes a single conversation can change your life, by opening your mind to possibilities never dreamed of. I was lucky to have such a conversation at a young age, quite unexpectedly. It happened when Peter told me how he planned to become a millionaire, retire early, and never work in a job again.

At the age of sixteen, I was trying to make sense of Marxism. My parents were both socialists, and I wanted to be one too. But the more I read about Marxism, the less sense it made. I was asking a lot of questions that my mother couldn't answer. She suggested that I speak to a man called Peter, who had previously been involved in the same political group as her.

When I met Peter, he was in his mid-twenties and I

was a teenager. He had a well-paid job in the City, London's financial center. I visited Peter at his small Greenwich apartment, where he showed me into a room he called his "library." Every wall had floor-to-ceiling shelving, stacked full with books.

Peter seemed to have read every important book I had heard of in the fields of philosophy, history, and politics. Whenever I borrowed one of these books in the years to come, I would find pages of his neatly written notes tucked inside the covers. He formed his own theories and viewpoints about everything he read, but he was unconcerned about publishing any of his ideas.

Peter was not a typical city worker. His favorite character from literature was Sherlock Holmes, whose demeanor he obviously emulated—he even smoked a pipe. He rarely socialized and was awkward around strangers, especially women. His favorite activity was discussing philosophy in an armchair in his library, with a glass of whiskey, surrounded by a fog of pipe smoke.

Peter had suffered an extremely harsh childhood in poverty. He was an orphan, adopted by violently abusive parents. His adoptive parents were ignorant and did not value education, but he had nonetheless succeeded in getting into Cambridge, one of the most exclusive universities in the country.

Over many late nights, many cigarettes for me, and many pipe refills for Peter, I questioned him about Marxism. Rather than defend his former ideology, Peter recognized fallacies in the arguments. He frankly acknowledged that ideas he had previously advocated were not just fallacious, but also incredibly destructive. As a result of our discussions, he abandoned Marxism once and for all, and I gave up on the idea of becoming a convert. We became good friends.

A couple of years after we met, Peter and I had the conversation that changed my life. By this time, Peter had left his city job and set up his own business. I learned a huge amount about entrepreneurship by talking to him about his venture. One night, sitting in his flat in Greenwich, I asked Peter what his goals in life were.

Peter told me that his goal was to become a millionaire and retire early. He intended to work extremely hard, create a profitable business, and make his fortune. As he spoke, I was impressed by his seriousness. He wasn't just dreaming about becoming a millionaire; he was planning it. I had never heard anyone admit to having such an ambitious life plan.

Everything Peter planned to do, he would accomplish through his own efforts. There are many opportunities for highly intelligent people like Peter to move into comfortable, protected jobs where they can live largely at everyone else's expense. My university professors provided examples of this lifestyle. In contrast, Peter was the most enterprising person I'd ever met. He would never compromise his ideas to fit into a cushy government job or to get grant money as an academic. He would build his own fortune and tell the world where to stick it.

Peter told me he planned to quit the rat race once he

had reached a net worth of £1 million. He believed in his ability to become a multimillionaire, but he didn't see any point in having such a goal. He calculated that a million would be enough money to give him the freedom to do whatever he wanted, which would probably be mostly reading, coming up with theories, and smoking his pipe in his armchair.

This part of his plan also left a deep impression on me. Peter was planning to change course radically. He intended to become a success in his chosen career and then simply quit and do something else. Everyone else I knew was working to find belonging and acceptance within some group. Peter didn't seem to care at all what others thought of him. He was making goals based on what would bring him personal fulfillment.

At the time, I was still trying to find a place for myself in the working world. I had never met anyone who planned to drop out of his career and redesign life on his own terms. Of course, I had met many people whose circumstances had forced them to find new ways to make ends meet, when they lost a job or were unsuccessful. But I'd never met someone planning to be a successful dropout.

Peter knew that it was up to him to create a great life for himself, regardless of his background. He saw it as his responsibility to realize the full potential of his character and to make the circumstances of his birth irrelevant. This attitude inspired me.

Our paths in life eventually diverged, as I will explain later. Nonetheless, Peter taught me what it means to take ownership of your life. He showed me what it means to free yourself. His example also suggested a time frame to accomplish financial independence: Peter was on track to reach early retirement some time in his mid-thirties.

About Me

That pivotal conversation with Peter was my first introduction to the idea of living a job-free life. I stopped thinking about how to find a good job and started thinking about how I could create the kind of life in which I didn't need one. Peter gave me encouragement and guidance, and he lent me money when I wanted to start my own business. I found my path to job freedom through entrepreneurship, when I founded a startup in 2000 called *Intelligent Space*.

Intelligent Space was a pedestrian movement consultancy. We advised architects, engineers, and developers on how to create better environments for pedestrians. We developed computer simulations that mapped where people are likely to walk, which is often not the same as where architects or engineers think they *should* walk.

I found the experience of building a business deeply fulfilling, even when it was stressful. Being my own boss was awesome. I slowly grew the business, and (with many missteps along the way) eventually achieved a high level of profitability. I wrote about the founding and growth of my business in my book, *Becoming an Entrepreneur*.[1]

From talking with Peter, I learned another way to think about the purpose of money. Money can buy freedom rather than comforts. You can use money to change your life, rather than let it control your life. Money can be a tool of personal liberation.

I achieved financial independence at the age of 35. I was able to do so because I sold my business to a large engineering company. I stayed on, working as a director for the company for three years, helping to integrate my business into their operation. At the end of that earn-out period, in 2010, I retired early at the age of 38.

Since I sold my business, my priority in life has been freedom. I have arranged my consumption habits and financial life around the goal of giving myself the freedom to do whatever I want with my day. I treasure never having to work on anything that I don't want to. I now live from passive investments as a private investor. I spend my time only on projects and activities that I feel enthusiastic about.

After I sold my business, I started a podcast called *The Voluntary Life*.[2] In the podcast I share my own experience of finding freedom through entrepreneurship, but I also interview others who have found freedom in different ways. Each person I've interviewed has their own story about how they are able to live every day as they choose.

The people I have interviewed have diverse lifestyles, but there is a common theme: they have all chosen different ways to live without a job. A job-free lifestyle means no longer having to work for anyone else. We are all masters of our own lives.

Job Free

There is nothing inherently exploitative about jobs. In fact, your job can serve to help build for a job-free future, as I will describe. I don't believe jobs are evil. It is just far more fulfilling to be your own boss and work for your dream, rather than have a boss and work for someone else's dream.

Many people would love to live a job-free life, but they have difficulty seeing how this could be a practical option for them. This difficulty is not surprising when you consider how we all learned about the working world.

Every teacher that I ever encountered in school or university was a lifelong employee. Those teachers conveyed their own assumptions about work to me over more than a decade of indoctrination. I bet your teachers gave you the same messages. It's time to unlearn your many years of employee conditioning. A job-free life is a realistic option for everyone, including you.

The simplest way to describe the benefit of a job-free life is this: you don't have to put up with any bullshit. If you're not dependent on someone else for a salary, it's easier to stand up for what you believe in. There are times when you might face moral challenges in a job. You may be asked to do something unethical by your boss, or to comply with (and tacitly condone) unprincipled practices by others. It is harder to stand up for your principles if you live paycheck to paycheck.

A reader captured this challenge in an email to me:

> I like to think I'm a moral person, but many times in my career, I've been forced to choose between unethical behavior and possibly losing my job. I handled this on a case by case manner where I had to weight the importance of the unethical behavior,

the likelihood of me being punished, the odds of me successfully elevating the issue to a superior, how much the unethical behavior would actually hurt the injured party, etc. In other words, my response was ambiguous and led to a lot of sleepless nights.

If you run your own business, you set your own standards. One customer might try to pressure you to do something dishonorable in return for their business. However, a healthy business is not dependent on any single customer to survive. It is much easier to refuse a customer than it is to refuse an employer.

Similarly, if you have multiple income streams as a freelancer, you will have more flexibility to decline work from any single source, if you believe that undertaking the work would violate your principles.

Even if you are still an employee, it is much easier to stand up for what you believe in if you are *working towards* job freedom. Employees who focus on saving for financial independence don't live paycheck to paycheck. Financial security makes it easier to say no to unethical requests. One of the best reasons to pursue financial independence is that it makes it much easier to say no to bad people.

Financial Independence

You may aspire to have the kind of lifestyle where you no longer have to work *at all*— having the financial freedom to do whatever you want with your time. This doesn't imply sitting on the couch watching TV all day. If you want to do lots of productive activities that you find fulfilling, more power to you. I've done all manner of things with my freedom, from launching a podcast, to writing books, to traveling the world.

Being financially free is not necessarily the same as being "rich" (whatever that means to you). In particular, it's not about having a high-consumption lifestyle. Instead, I define financial freedom in terms of the length of time you have ahead of you before you have to work in a job that you don't enjoy. The more time you have, the freer you are to do whatever you want with your life.

The objective is not to stop doing anything productive; it is to stop doing work that you don't *want* to do. My aim is to spend time only on activities and projects that inspire my wildest enthusiasm. My goal is to spend every precious moment of life in ways that I find fulfilling and that are aligned with my values.

Financial independence is a great basis for a job-free life, but not the only basis. You don't have to be financially independent in order to live job free. You have options.

Who This Book Is For

This book is for you if you want to create a job-free life for yourself. You don't need a detailed background in business or personal finance in order to understand the contents of this book. I have avoided jargon as much as possible.

Many books advocate specific plans for adopting the *best* lifestyle. Such books provide a set of instructions for you to follow the example set by the author. This book is different. My purpose is not to convince you to follow the same path as I did.

This book is unique in providing a framework for understanding the different options for job-free living. I explain and contrast the various job-free lifestyles. I suggest ways to use each approach and choose a lifestyle that best suits you. I provide further resources that you can explore in more detail.

A job-free life is possible and you have options about how to achieve it. When you understand the options, you can choose a path that best suits your talents and preferences.

If you are just beginning your journey to job freedom, you will get an overview of the entire journey ahead and all the options available. However, even if you already know a lot about one approach to creating a job-free life, you will gain an understanding of the alternatives that could also serve you.

The Book in a Nutshell

As I interviewed job-free people on my podcast, I began to spot a pattern I had not seen described before. Each person's route to freedom was unique, but they all seemed to fit one of four essential strategies.

Strategy 1: Save your way to a job-free life. Extreme savers aim to put away enough money to live from their investment returns indefinitely, so that they can retire early and devote their time to finding fulfillment in any way they choose. They do this by practicing radical frugality, saving the majority of their income for about 10 years so they can live the rest of their lives on their terms, while minimizing their expenses. I explain this approach in Chapter One, "Extreme Saving."

Strategy 2: Earn money outside a regular job, doing what you love. Unjobbers earn money from multiple income sources outside a job, such as freelancing or side businesses. They choose enjoyable work that gives them more freedom. In order to make this lifestyle feasible, they often live far more frugally than the mainstream consumption culture. This is the subject of Chapter Two, "Unjobbing."

Strategy 3: Create a business that supports your lifestyle. People following this strategy aim to design a business that requires so little of their time that they can work as much as they please and spend the rest of their time doing whatever gives them fulfillment. Chapter Three, "Lifestyle Businesses," is about how to support your freedom by using a business that pays your way.

Strategy 4: Build a business to achieve financial independence. Whereas lifestyle entrepreneurs use a business to provide income, startup entrepreneurs aim to build capital value in a business that they can one day sell. This is the subject of Chapter Four, "Startups."

I illustrate each of these four strategies with stories of real people who have chosen each route to job freedom. I've tried to choose people who represent examples of one particular route, but in reality many people use a combination of more than one strategy. You too can combine these different strategies and choose aspects of each. There is no need to choose one of the four ways to the exclusion of all the others. However, it helps to identify the four basic strategies separately.

I've also provided an appendix on investing, because the practical issues related to investing are relevant to many of the strategies for achieving job freedom.

You can choose a path to job freedom that suits your preferences and circumstances. When you understand the four options available, you can design your own path to freedom based on the building blocks provided by these four ways. Chapter Five, "Choosing a Job-Free Lifestyle," provides suggestions about how you can take the different lifestyle paths open to you and choose from them.

Creating a job-free life is not just a practical challenge. Chapter Six, "The Psychological Challenge," identifies three key mental aspects of your journey. **Outside a job, it's up to you to build a community, create structure for yourself, and find purpose in your life.**

Peter taught me that I can only be as free as I choose to make myself. Let's explore four strategies that you can use to free yourself.

CHAPTER ONE

Extreme Saving

There is a dignity in the very effort to save with a worthy purpose. ... It produces a well-regulated mind; it gives prudence a triumph over extravagance; it gives virtue the mastery over vice; it puts the passions under control; it drives away care; it secures comfort. Saved money, however little, will serve to dry up many a tear—will ward off many sorrows and heartburnings, which otherwise might prey upon us.
—Samuel Smiles, 1875

Joe Dominguez's Story

Joe Dominguez was born in Harlem in the 1930s. He made it to Wall Street, where he got a well-paid job as an investment analyst. He used his high income to save as much money as he could. By the age of thirty, he had saved the equivalent in today's money of over $400,000. At that point, he quit his job and lived from the interest on his savings. The interest income was modest, but he made it work by maintaining an extremely frugal lifestyle. He did not have any of the high-roller spending habits that you might expect from someone with a career on Wall Street. In fact, he made it his life's work to show others how saving and frugality could help them achieve financial independence.

Joe never worked for money again after he quit his Wall Street job. He used his financial freedom to devote himself to projects that he found fulfilling. Together with his partner, Vicki Robin, he wrote a best-selling book called *Your Money or Your Life*[3] that explained his approach to achieving financial independence. All the profits from the book went into a charitable foundation with a mission to provide financial education for ordinary people.

Joe died from cancer in 1997, at the age of 58. Imagine what a different life he would have had if, instead of retiring early, he had continued to work on Wall Street. If he had pursued a more traditional Wall Street career, he might have spent his remaining 28 years amassing a bigger and bigger fortune and spending it on the momentary pleasures of a consumption-oriented lifestyle. Instead, he spent those years doing what was most fulfilling to him: enjoying life, spreading the message of financial independence, and helping millions of people to free themselves from financial worries. Which life would you prefer?

Although he did not use these words, I call the approach that Joe pioneered "extreme saving." This chapter explains the extreme saving strategy for achieving job freedom.

How Extreme Saving Works

Extreme saving involves a six-point strategy:
1. Get a decently paid job.
2. Adopt frugality as a central part of your lifestyle to

enable you to save the majority of your income (aim for 75 percent).
3. Begin investing your savings as soon as possible, to allow maximum time for compound interest and capital accumulation to work in your benefit.
4. Minimize investment costs by managing your money yourself and using low-cost investment vehicles. The lower your expenses, the higher your investment returns (and the more to compound).
5. Minimize taxes by using tax-deferred accounts (and any other legitimate minimization techniques). Minimizing taxes also gives more chance for compounding to work.
6. When you reach the point of financial independence, quit your job and live from your investments.

Here's a way to summarize the lifestyle of extreme saving: as you progress in your career, don't increase your consumption. In other words, as you earn more money, continue to live like a student. Then save all that additional money in a tax-efficient, low-expense way. The key challenge for extreme savers is sticking to a lifestyle that allows them to save a large proportion of their income. If you can stick to the saving, the remaining steps are relatively straightforward.

Employment and Extreme Saving

Unlike other approaches to living a job-free life, extreme savers usually work as full-time employees for many years. It makes sense for them to hold full-time jobs because the strategy requires a steady accumulation of savings, and a job can give you the steady income to save from. Most of the extreme savers I have interviewed were full-time employees during their income-earning years.

Justin, an early retiree who writes the blog *Root of Good*,[4] is an example of someone who used full-time employment as a means to early retirement, not as a source of fulfillment in itself. During the accumulation phase, he protected his free time outside work in order to gain fulfillment from family time and personal projects. Here is how Justin explained his approach to me:

> I was kind of picky in terms of my career, because I didn't want to work really hard. I wanted to have plenty of free time. But I think I was also smart, in the sense that I [made decisions based on the bigger picture of what work is for]. ... We had a business relationship: they paid me money in exchange for me doing awesome things for them. And so I focused on making sure that I was compensated appropriately and when it was time to go somewhere else and get rewarded, I made that choice.

Many other early retirees used full-time employment as the source of their savings. As previously mentioned, Joe Dominguez was a full-time employee. Jeremy and Winnie, who write the blog *Go Curry Cracker*[5], were full-time employees during their accumulation phase. Jacob Lund Fisker is an early retiree who runs a blog called *Early Retirement Extreme* [6] and has also published a book of the same name.[7] He is a former academic who was able to achieve financial independence in his thirties by saving more than 75 percent of his university income.

Amy Dacyczyn (pronounced "decision") is another

example of someone who took the intensive saver approach based on an employee income. She published a newsletter in the 1990s called *The Tightwad Gazette*, now available as a book.[8] Dacyczyn was a homemaker with various side projects that brought in income, but her husband was a full-time employee. As a household, they saved money based largely on his salary. When they got married in the early 1980s, they had only $1,500 in savings. In seven years, they had four children and saved $49,000—all from one income, which at that time was under $30,000 a year.[9]

Pete, who runs an entertaining blog called *Mr. Money Mustache*,[10] is another early retiree who used full-time employment as his income vehicle. He worked as a tech industry employee and retired in his early thirties. He lives from investments he accumulated using extreme saving.

How Important Is Your Income Level?

The higher your income, the easier it will be to pursue extreme saving. Many of the extreme savers I have interviewed were in relatively high-paying jobs in technical fields. Pete (from *Mr. Money Mustache*), Jeremy (from *Go Curry Cracker*), and Justin (from *Root of Good*) were all engineers.

However, the strategy is not limited to those with high-paying jobs. Mike and Lauren are a husband and wife team who run a website[11] and a YouTube channel[12] describing their journey to financial freedom. They are on track to reach financial independence by the age of 30. They are pursuing this goal without the benefit of especially high-paying jobs. Mike and Lauren described their background to me:

> We never received any inheritance or even a major bonus or anything at work that would have contributed a significant chunk. ... We both just have regular full-time jobs. ... We earn around $60,000 a year combined—that's with two full-time jobs, and we both have side projects that we're working on. The median household income in the United States is somewhere between $50,000 and $55,000, so we're just normal earners. This is definitely something that normal people can do.[13]

We live in such a high-consumption culture that there are always opportunities to be more frugal. Many saving measures will have no impact on your happiness. We could all save more money and still have a fulfilled and enjoyable life because the predominant lifestyle is so financially inefficient.

Saving the Majority of Your Income

Extreme saving involves significant lifestyle changes. The approach requires saving the majority of your income on an ongoing basis. At a minimum, you save 50 percent of your earnings. Ideally, you save 75 percent or more. Given various assumptions, if you save over 50 percent of your income and could live sustainably from the remaining amount, then you could retire in about 16 years. If you save 75 percent of your income, then you could retire in about eight years.[14]

Jeremy and Winnie, the husband and wife team behind *Go Curry Cracker*, used the approach of extreme saving to reach financial independence over the course of 10 years. They are early retirees who spend their time permanently traveling. As they explore the world, they share their experiences and a breakdown of their financial expenses on their blog.

When I interviewed Jeremy, he described their ten years of saving:

> During that time period we were saving upwards of 70 percent or so [of our income]. Then in the last couple of years, our portfolio was basically supporting our lifestyle, so 100 percent of our after-tax income was going into our savings. The straight-up math of it works out that if you are doing a typical 10 percent savings rate, you need to work nine years before you have enough put away to fund one year of your current lifestyle. Whereas, if you are saving 90 percent, then after one year of work you've saved nine years worth of living expenses. Something pretty magical starts to happen in the compounding when you get above the 50 to 60 percent savings rate.[15]

Lowering Expenses Provides Easy Wins

You can increase savings both by increasing your income and by reducing your expenses. The easy wins for savers usually come from reducing expenses. Therefore, once they have a reasonable income in place, extreme savers tend to focus more on reducing expenses.

You have more control over expenses than you do over income. Your pay partly depends on factors outside your control, such as the profitability of your employer's business, or the economic climate. In contrast, your personal expenditures are entirely within your control. You can choose to be more frugal with your spending, without needing any action on the part of your employer.

The higher your income level, the more effective will be lowering expenses compared to increasing income. As you increase your income, it becomes harder to minimize taxes because you move into progressively higher tax brackets. You can mitigate tax increases to a certain extent by using tax-deferred accounts, but this also locks up your money.

Thomas J. Stanley studied first-generation millionaire households in the United States for his book *The Millionaire Next Door*.[16] His research led him to conclude that spending choices are more important than income for developing wealth:

> People think that as long as they generate high incomes, wealth will surely follow. Nothing could be further from the truth. It so happens, in fact, that for purposes of building wealth ... once you are in a high income bracket it matters less how much more you make than what you do with what you already have.[17]

As an employee, you may be required to take on more job-related expenses in order to increase your income. Working for someone else may also involve spending time away from your family or other pursuits. Most importantly, making more money will not increase your wealth at all if you simply spend it on more consumption items. Gaining conscious control of your spending, therefore, matters more than increasing income.

Many extreme savers prefer to focus on minimizing expenses rather than increasing income, as this gives them more control and freedom of choice. Justin from *Root of Good* described his approach to getting more income versus saving more:

> In terms of the day-to-day, I always wanted that 40-hour per week job. I didn't want to have a long commute or lots of travel. So my income probably suffered because of it, but that extra little bit of money that I could have made probably would not have made a

> lot of difference in terms of happiness long-term. I put more effort into saving money ... economizing where I could, researching purchases and that sort of thing.[18]

Frugality not only helps you increase your savings rate, it also decreases the target amount of savings that you need for financial independence. As you reduce your living expenses, you reduce the amount of wealth needed to live from as an early retiree. I provide an overview of the technical issues regarding this subject in Appendix: About Investing.

Key Expenses to Target for Saving

Extreme saving is not about agonizing over every purchase. Rather, it is about having a sustainable strategy for saving on the biggest ongoing expenses. If you know where your money goes, then you are able to prioritize your cost cutting to those areas that will give you the most benefit.

Extreme savers focus their saving efforts on those expenses that tend to eat up the biggest part of a budget. As Mike from *Mike And Lauren* explained, "There are three major areas where the bulk of your spending is probably going: it's going to your housing, your transportation, and your food, in that order."[19] Jeremy from *Go Curry Cracker* described how he and his wife Winnie adopted the same approach to prioritizing: "Our main three savings approaches are what give people 80 percent of the benefit—it's where most of the money goes—between housing, transportation, and food."[20]

Housing

Most people could achieve big savings in their housing expenditure because house choice has become a vehicle for the expression of social status and lifestyle aspirations. Everyone needs a decent shelter in a location with access to amenities. Housing provides this, but it is also a bucket for a lot of discretionary spending beyond such basic needs. That discretionary spending often goes into buying larger properties, but it can also go into remodeling kitchens or other kinds of upgrading.

Extreme savers don't use criteria like social status when choosing their homes. Instead, they think of a house as simply a consumption expenditure. As with all other forms of consumption, they try to spend as frugally as possible. Jeremy from *Go Curry Cracker* described how he and his wife's housing choice helped them save:

> While many of my coworkers were living in 3,000-square-foot homes that were being paid for with a large mortgage from dual-income families, we were living in a 900-square-foot apartment in a 1930s-era building. I don't feel like we'd lacked anything because we weren't in a 3,000-square-foot house. If anything, we didn't have to paint, we didn't have to mow the lawn. ... If we spend 90 percent of the time in several hundred square feet, why heat and cool and maintain the other several thousand that some Americans live in? So our costs were substantially less than [those of] our peers.[21]

I followed a similar approach when it came to my own housing choices. I lived in a small studio apartment until my late thirties. I always rented and did not own any property until after I had sold my business. I never had a mortgage. One consequence of this choice was that I was able to use the money that I saved on housing to invest in my business.

Transportation

Transportation is another expense category that offers big opportunities for saving. In particular, finding alternatives to a car is a great way to improve your finances. A car is an expensive purchase that begins depreciating the moment you buy it. It sits unused most of the time, but requires constant spending on fuel, road taxes, maintenance, parking, and other expenses.

Some people see the purchase of a nice car as the reward they can give themselves for all the stress and hassle of being stuck in a job they dislike. In contrast, extreme savers view transportation as a logistical problem and the ownership of a car as merely one possible solution to this problem. If they need a car, extreme savers will opt to purchases a $5,000 used car rather than the $60,000 new luxury car. Thereby, they make immediate savings on the initial purchases and pay far less for taxes and insurance.

Many alternative forms of transportation are more economical than private car ownership, such as using public transportation, riding a bicycle, or even joining a car club. Many extreme savers deliberately choose to live in locations that will enable them to rely on public transportation or—even better—walking and cycling. Here is how Jeremy from *Go Curry Cracker* described his strategy for transportation:

> Transportation-wise, we very actively found the apartment where we lived. We were a block from the grocery store. We were across the street from a weekly farmers market. We were five blocks from the public library. We were on a main thoroughfare for public transit. I could walk downstairs and get on a bus that would take me to the office. We didn't have a car and most days I commuted to work by bicycle.[22]

If you live in a high-density town or city, you can consider going car-free entirely. I have deliberately never owned a car. I avoid all the hassle of parking, maintenance, taxes, insurance, and the host of minor errands that go with car ownership. I get more exercise by walking and I can always rent a car if I need one.

This is only possible if you deliberately choose to live in a place that has good transportation links and a dense network of streets. However, I consider walkable neighborhoods to offer the best quality of life that urban living affords. Far from being a sacrifice, I see not owning a car as a positive lifestyle choice.

Food

There is a huge opportunity to save money on food expenditure by not eating out as much. Eating in restaurants is another example of an expenditure that can feel like a psychological reward for all the hard work that you do in a full-time job. After working hard all day, the temptation is to "treat yourself" by going out for a meal at a restaurant in the evening. Annual restaurant visits per capita in the US rose from 153 in 1991 to 178 in 2001 (suggesting that people were eating out every other day on average).[23]

Another example is the small eating out that most employees do every day when they get their lunch from a takeout restaurant or cafe. Paying for lunch seems like a negligible cost, but such expenses add up and can have a big impact on your annual expenditure.

Extreme savers cook for themselves and thereby save on these expenses. Jeremy from *Go Curry Cracker* told me about how he and Winnie changed their spending habits on food:

> There was a period where Winnie was working through a French and Italian cookbook and we got to the point when we thought, why go out to eat when we are having these amazing meals at home for a fraction of the price? Winnie's cooking skills rival many Michelin-star chefs. Over the course of a few years, she invested in that and decided, "I'm going to make great food at home for a reasonable price."[24]

Extreme Savers and Taxes

Extreme savers try to minimize their tax burden by using tax-sheltered savings accounts whenever possible. There can be limits to this approach, depending on the laws in your country. Most governments limit the amount of money you can put into tax-sheltered accounts each year.[25] There are also limits on the total amount of money you can shelter from taxes in a retirement account.[26] These limits are also subject to change over time, for example, the UK lowered the maximum tax-free amount for pensions recently[27]. You may not be able to rely on tax-sheltered savings accounts as part of your extreme saving strategy in the future.

Tax-sheltered accounts do not give employees as much flexibility to minimize taxes as entrepreneurs have through business ownership. One obvious problem with retirement accounts is that you usually cannot access your funds until you reach a minimum age, which varies by country but is usually in your mid-fifties. If you plan to retire early—say in your mid-thirties—then you have two decades in which you might not be able to access the majority of your funds.

There are sometimes legitimate ways around this constraint. Joshua Sheats is a former financial advisor who now runs the *Radical Personal Finance*[28] podcast. He told me about a technique used in the United States called a "back-door Roth IRA." Using this technique, you may be able to withdraw some of your US retirement funds earlier without incurring additional taxes.[29] Consult your accountant or registered tax advisor in your own country to get advice on how the most recent tax laws apply to your circumstances.

In short, the use of tax-deferred accounts limits what you can do with your money. These limitations can involve removing access to your money for many years, as is the case in most countries, or reducing access significantly but not completely—as is the case in the US. Locking up your funds in retirement accounts limits your flexibility and your ability to use your resources.

The Power of Compound Interest

The success of the extreme saving strategy is not solely based on saving a large amount. It also depends on utilizing the power of compound interest. Your first saved money earns some interest. Then both the initial capital and the interest together earn even more interest, and so on: it compounds.

Many people are unaware of the power that compounding interest has for increasing your savings. As an example, if you save $3,000 every year from the age of 21, by the time you are 65, you would have contributed just over $100k into savings. However, if those savings were earning 8% as investments, then with compound interest, your amount saved would have grown to over $1m.

Intensive savers take advantage of compound interest by starting to save early in their careers so that the compounding has more time to work. They also save as much of their income each year as they can, so that there is more money to compound.

Extreme Saving and Investing

Economic conditions have changed a lot since Joe Dominguez retired early using extreme saving. Most of his early retirement occurred during the long boom period of the 1980s and 1990s, which now looks like a golden age for retirees. He was able to put all his savings in treasury bonds and live from the interest.

We live in very different times. Central banks the world over are forcing interest rates to artificially low levels. If you were to follow Joe's investment strategy in these conditions, you would probably not make enough money to cover the ravaging effects of inflation. You also can't rely on the stock market to return the enormous profits it did during the 1980s and 1990s.

Extreme savers have adopted various alternative investment portfolios in response to changing market conditions. Although there are different schools of thought, most extreme savers adopt some form of *passive investing* portfolio for their investments. This approach is summarized in Appendix: About Investing.

One common aspect of investment strategy that extreme savers agree on is the importance of minimizing investment costs. Such costs can significantly lower your returns in both good and bad markets, so efforts to save on these expenses are worthwhile. Most intensive savers manage their investments themselves and use low-cost index funds, instead of actively managed funds that charge high fees.

Extreme savers use various guidelines to calculate when they have saved enough to be able to live from their investments. One of the most important guidelines is known as the f*our percent rule,* which I cover in the appendix. Once extreme savers have built up enough money to live from their investments, they can retire early and do whatever they want with their time.

Things to Consider About Extreme Saving

Extreme saving is probably the lowest-risk strategy for achieving a job-free life. If you have the discipline to implement the lifestyle changes, you can become financially independent in about 10 years. It's a much more straightforward strategy than becoming an entrepreneur. You don't need to address the challenges of creating a profitable business. You just have to hold down your job and do the saving.

The downside of this approach is that you probably need to stay in a job for perhaps a decade while you save, for the reasons explained in this chapter. If a job-free life is your goal, then this is certainly a disadvantage. I have always found entrepreneurship far more enjoyable for the personal freedom it gives me. If you don't mind working for someone else for 10 years, perhaps this does not matter to you.

It's worth considering the consequences of a heavy reliance on retirement accounts for investing purposes, if you want to pursue this approach. As discussed, this creates practical problems for early retirement because it limits your access to your money. It also reduces your flexibility to change plans. Should you decide that you would like to start a business after all, you may not have the flexibility to access your funds.

Relying on retirement accounts as a key part of your investment strategy opens you up to sovereign risk. Governments have a habit of stealing money from pension funds when State finances are tight. For example, Argentina confiscated $3.2 billion of private pension savings in 2001 and $30 billion of pension fund assets in 2008, to fund its current spending.[30] This problem is not limited to Argentina. In the last six years, governments have confiscated private pension funds to some extent in Ireland, Poland, France,[31] Bolivia,[32] Hungary, Portugal, Bulgaria, and Russia.[33]

In the worst-case scenario, you might work a lifetime to

build up your retirement savings only to find that your funds have been confiscated by a bankrupt government. Of course, bankrupt governments are a risk to anyone, but the extreme savers are more reliant on retirement accounts than people following any other strategy for escaping the rat race. If you want to pursue this approach, you have to trust that your retirement funds will still be there when you need them.

Further Resources On Extreme Saving

Podcast Episodes

You can hear the interviews mentioned in this chapter in the following episodes of *The Voluntary Life*:

Episode 162—Spend Little, Save More, Travel the World: Interview with Go Curry Cracker[34]

Episode 164—We Plan To Retire At 30: Interview with Mike and Lauren[35]

Episode 166—Retired at 33: Interview with Justin from Root of Good[36]

Episode 209—Tax Strategies And Financial Freedom Part 1 (Interview With Joshua Sheats)[37]

Books

I suggest Joe Dominguez's original book, *Your Money or Your Life,* as a good introduction to extreme saving. The later edition by his coauthor Vicki Robin[38] is more relevant for contemporary economic conditions. A more recent book, *Early Retirement Extreme*, by Jacob Lund Fisker,[39] presents an updated approach to extreme saving.

An out-of-print book by Paul Terhorst called *Cashing In On The American Dream*[40] may be of interest if you want to read an early example of extreme saving with a high income (although the investment examples in the book are all very out of date).

See also Appendix A: About Investing for more resources on the investment side of extreme saving.

Websites

Jacob Lund Fisker has a website at earlyretirementextreme.com where you can connect to other extreme savers. Mr.s Money Mustache also has an active community at mrmoneymoustache.com.

CHAPTER TWO
Unjobbing

We act as though comfort and luxury were the chief requirements of life, when all that we need to make us happy is something to be enthusiastic about.
—Charles Kingsley

Michael Fogler's Story

Michael Fogler is a classical guitarist. In the 1970s, when he was in college, he wanted to become a teacher. For many years after graduation, he tried to secure a faculty teaching position. As you might imagine, there were not many classical-guitar teaching positions in universities. For a long time, Michael took odd jobs on the side to support himself while he tried to build a career. He thought that in order to succeed in life, he would have to get the kind of job his parents and teachers had always expected of him.

As time went by, he began to realize he'd been supporting himself by doing various things for many years, and had never had a full-time job. He also realized that he was happy about this because he didn't want a full-time job. He decided to stop trying to get one and to embrace life without a regular job.

He resolved to work only on things that were in true accord with his values. So he became a peace activist and did various other things that were meaningful to him. In order to sustain this lifestyle, Michael chose to live extremely frugally. He minimized his expenses far beyond the norm of the culture around him.

In the 1990s, Michael wrote a book called *Unjobbing: The Adult Liberation Handbook*,[41] explaining how to adopt this lifestyle. I tracked Michael down and interviewed him. He turned out to be a friendly, gentle character. You can hear him explain the approach in episode 34 of *The Voluntary Life*.[42]

In his book, Michael defined unjobbing as "letting go of the preoccupation with, and self-inflicted domination and life consumption by, an 'occupation,' while consciously and joyfully reclaiming life." [43]

Other Unjobbers

Many people have developed lifestyles similar to the unjobbing concept described by Michael. Linda Breen Pierce writes about simplifying your lifestyle and consumption habits, which many consider an integral part of unjobbing. She left a career as a corporate lawyer to pursue a life of voluntary simplicity in the 1990s. She undertook a study of 211 people who made similar choices and summarized her findings in the book *Choosing Simplicity*.[44]

Elliott Hulse is a strength trainer and YouTube personality[45] with a mission to help others "become the strongest possible versions of themselves" physically and mentally. Although his personal style is very different to that of the gentle, peace activist Michael Fogler, I see many similarities in the approach that Elliott Hulse developed. Elliott created a Non-job Manifesto,[46] embodying his version of unjobbing principles.

Elliott emphasizes the link between living more authentically and being able to get paid for your work. Your authentic passion is your unique selling point—it is the reason that people will take interest in your business. Therefore, your personal development is integral to the commercial viability of activities that you find fulfilling. Here is how Elliott described it to me:

> You are probably going to really suck in the beginning, but you need to suck, because that is the soil through which the greater version of you—the one that's going to earn—comes from. People come to you for your expertise but they stay with you because of the character or the personality that is presenting it. ... You've got to be more expansive than just your expertise. It doesn't mean you've got to learn new things, but what you've got to do is share your experiences beyond that expertise in order for people to get to know, like, and trust you.[47]

The Mindset Behind Unjobbing

Unjobbing is a way to live a job-free lifestyle without having achieved financial independence. Rather than aiming to retire early, unjobbers seek to redesign their working lives to remove the aspects of work they don't feel fulfilled by doing. In return, they recognize that they will not receive many of the benefits that regular employees receive. This trade-off is one that unjobbers are willing to take.

The concept of unjobbing is to create your own program for workplace fulfillment by creating your own work. Instead of asking, "How can I find a great job?" it starts with the question, "How can I make money doing something I find fulfilling?"

Unjobbers want to work without commuting, fixed hours, and the other typical disadvantages of many jobs. Usually, they will have to forgo some money and security of income to achieve the work experience they want.

Unjobbing is closer to an entrepreneur's outlook than it is to an employee's outlook, although not all unjobbers choose to become business owners. Many unjobbers are freelancers or part-time employees with multiple income streams.

From the unjobber's perspective, if you don't feel fulfilled in your working life, then it is your responsibility to do something about it. After all, only you can create the conditions of your own fulfillment.

The cultural conditioning towards employment is so strong that people tend to be oblivious to the possibility of designing their own working life. Redesigning your working life for maximum fulfillment leads you to make choices outside traditional career paths. The unquestioned norm is a career comprised of employee positions; most people don't think about the alternatives open to them. In Michael Fogler's view, the very idea of "career" can be a hindrance itself, as it puts many people on paths that are not fulfilling. He writes:

> This was the message—and it was a strong one—handed to us by

society at large through our parents. The message was clearly this: "Yes, you should try to be happy and fulfilled, but keep your life focused on your career."[48]

Unjobbing is incompatible with the idea of spending years of your life doing things you don't want to do, in order to eventually "make it." Unjobbers choose not to concern themselves with how a life choice might look on their résumé or curriculum vitae. Instead, their criterion for choosing what to do is whether they love doing it.

How Unjobbing Works

Unjobbers do not make career choices that require them to defer happiness for the sake of high pay. Instead, unjobbers seek to hack their working lives—to find a way to do only the things that they love. If you choose a life working only on projects you love, then it doesn't feel like work. You would do it for free. But the question is, how do you hack your work to achieve this?

Unfortunately, working on things you love often doesn't pay well. Unjobbing usually has the following consequences:

- You will probably earn much less income—at least at first—if you don't earn money from a typical job.
- You are unlikely to have the same predictability of income that goes with a typical job.
- You probably will not find an employer who is willing to redesign a job for you in such a radical way that it meets all your requirements and still gives you enough income for a typical consumption lifestyle.

Unjobbers have to develop a strategy to deal with these consequences. How can you free yourself of the need for a significant chunk of income, so you have more flexibility in deciding how to earn money? How can you replace a job with income from other sources? Typically, the unjobbing strategy comprises three aspects:

1. **Voluntary simplicity:** Given the possibility of lower income, unjobbers usually seek to radically cut their spending and use far fewer resources. As a start, they avoid many expenses related to a typical job. The biggest potential comes from adopting a minimalist lifestyle that emphasizes simplicity.
2. **Frugal living:** Given the lower predictability of income, unjobbers design their lives for far greater efficiency in their use of resources. They pursue a lifestyle of extreme frugality.
3. **Multiple income streams:** Multiple income streams often enable unjobbers to have a more entrepreneurial approach to earning money from various side hustles.

Voluntary Simplicity

Since the most obvious downside of not doing work that you dislike is the lowering of your income, unjobbing forces you to reevaluate your spending patterns. The activities you love doing may not make much money in the marketplace. If you want to support yourself from such activities, you may have to live more frugally. For many people taking this approach, the consequence is that they live a lifestyle of voluntary

Job Free

simplicity, at least in the short term.

You may have to do with less material comfort in order to create the life you want, especially in the early stages while you are getting started. This is how Elliot Hulse described the mindset:

> You don't need an iPhone and cable TV in your home. You don't need a Mercedes-Benz. You don't need fashion designer clothing. You don't need to eat expensive food. You need a little bit of food for your belly—so that your mind can think and your body can grow and be healthy—and then you go to work. What's wrong with living in your car? I was never afraid to live in my car. I told my wife, "Look, if this doesn't work, there might come a point where we are going to live in my car." We had all sorts of plans for the first bill that we were not going to pay. We had it all planned out, and not because I was expecting failure, but because I wasn't going to stop. ... The only thing stopping most people when it comes to the whole money situation is that they don't realize that they can live on far less than they think they need.[49]

Some people see a lifestyle of voluntary simplicity as a positive benefit in itself. They take an approach of conscious minimalism, deliberately choosing to sell or get rid of as many possessions as possible. In doing so, they have less stuff to maintain, and they recover value from possessions that they don't really need. Jorja Levitt is an entrepreneur and stay-at-home mother of four living in Las Vegas. When I interviewed Jorja on *The Voluntary Life*, she described her own journey to simplification:

> Five years ago, I decided to become an entrepreneur and work for myself. In that process, working from home, I discovered that I had a lot of assets in my house that I could convert into cash while I was starting my own business. I pretty much sold anything excess [to our needs]. This allowed me to stay home, to start my career, and to be with my four children. It gave me some flexibility and it was a great way to bring in extra income while I was doing

> my own business. What I really noticed, as I did this, was that I felt freer. I wasn't bogged down by trying to get things repaired, or trying to find a place to store things when I wasn't using them. ... I really took pride in the fact that we had a place for all our stuff—there wasn't anything just lingering around. If it didn't have a place, then we didn't need it. How many of us have actually just lost something because we have so much stuff that we don't even know where it is if we went to go look for it? Normally my rule of thumb [is that I get rid of something] if I haven't used it in the last year ... and if I can easily replace it. So I have a few things that I wouldn't get rid of, like the dishes that my grandmother gave me, but I don't hold on to a lot of other things. I don't collect anything. I tell people I collect money. I can find a place for that easily![50]

Simplification is a strategy that may help you transition to unjobbing, but you don't necessarily have to pursue voluntary simplicity to pursue unjobbing. If you manage to find income-generating activities that you love, which also happen to pay well, more power to you.

Frugal Living

Unjobbers focus on living frugally for slightly different reasons from those of extreme savers. Extreme savers use frugality to reach financial independence, at which point they can do whatever they like to find fulfillment. In contrast, unjobbers use frugality to enable them to pursue work that they find fulfilling.

Unjobbers are critical of mainstream spending habits, because they see these habits as a barrier to freedom in work. For many people, the purpose of work is to fund a high-consumption lifestyle. For those focused on consumption, the goal is to own a big house, or drive a nice car. But a high-consumption lifestyle usually reduces your freedom. You will most likely incur debts and struggle with ongoing payments in order to finance that lifestyle.

Unjobbers reject high-consumption spending habits, especially on key areas such as housing. Buying a home is just the first rung on a "property ladder" of spending for many people. The standard pattern is to upgrade your home regularly throughout your life, piling more of your money into housing expenditure. Every time you trade up your property, you end up spending a lot of money.

Purchasing a house usually involves significant debt that, until recently, most people didn't believe was a risk at all. The property bubble of the early 2000s led many to believe buying a house with a mortgage was a sure bet: a house's value could never fall. The last housing market crash proved this belief to be disastrously mistaken. As Doug French writes in his book, *Walk Away*:

> It seems like a crazy idea now, but many financial advisors during the boom told anyone who would listen that they shouldn't pay off or even pay down their mortgage debt. Not only should everyone own a home, but everyone should have a mortgage and no one should ever pay it off. The conventional wisdom, built up from decades of government support for home ownership, was that housing prices could never fall. Yet prices did fall. In the wake of the great recession after 2008, prices plummeted so far that many people found themselves in negative equity—owing more on the mortgage than the value of their home. First American Core Logic estimated that nearly a third of all mortgages (32.3 percent) were under water in June of 2009. ... That's 15.2 million loans, and the negative equity position totaled $3.4 trillion.[51]

Many unjobbers choose a lifestyle that removes the stress of keeping up with large mortgage debts. They find cheaper housing choices, such as living in a tiny house. Jacki

Rigoni writes the blog *Post-Consumer Life*.[52] She lived in a million-dollar home until she and her family understood the negative impact it had on their lives. They sold the home and moved to a plot of land where they could build their own tiny house. Jacki described how she experienced the house-spending trap:

> A million-dollar home sounds ridiculous, but we were living in The San Francisco Bay Area. Everybody's living ridiculously here. A million-dollar home is the norm. Once we got married, we started down the same path as everybody else. We both had good jobs—I'm a freelance copywriter and my husband Maurizio is an electrician—so we were making good money, making home payments, and doing the things that everybody else around us did. But it was just crazy. You're driving your kids here and there, you're trying to work, you're trying to pay the bills, you barely have time for each other, you wave hello in passing. Gradually, we realized that it was not us and that there must be something better. ... Up front in a mortgage you're mostly paying interest, so after paying thousands of dollars each month in mortgage, we were barely owners of a mere part of that home. Nobody really owns their own home until they are old (if ever) because everyone keeps on refinancing and resetting the clock. A hundred years ago, everyone made their own home, or they would rent. It's really a new phenomenon that all of us are working our butts off to pay a mortgage.

Jacki told me about her transition, giving up a million-dollar mortgage to live in a tiny home free of debt:

> As my kids were getting older, I felt like my time with my kids was like trying to cup water in your hands: you're squeezing your fingers together tight to keep all that water in, but slowly it's dripping out. My time with my kids was getting away from me. We realized that what we really wanted was space to breathe, room to run around, time with our kids, and freedom to not have to run into work every day and spend the prime waking hours doing [a job] that was the main goal of getting up every morning. ... We found a piece of land that we would be able to buy with what we could get out of the sale of our house. After we packed up the

last of our stuff and drove away from that home, we were all doing this collective happy dance. It just felt so liberating. You don't even realize how oppressive that debt is until you're actually free of it. [53]

Jacki and her family now live debt free on their own property. They have chosen to reduce their housing requirements significantly in order to benefit from the resulting freedom. It is a much simpler style of life without the stress that comes with climbing the property ladder.

As well as lowering your overall expenses, there are many opportunities to make every dollar you spend go further. By making your spending more efficient and effective, you further reduce your future expenses.

Multiple Income Streams

One of the most self-limiting beliefs is to classify yourself as an employee. If you think of yourself as part of an employee class, then you will believe your advancement is largely at the mercy of an employer class. This is only true if you make it so. The reality is that economic roles can be far more fluid. There are many ways of making a living outside a pure employee role. As the economist Ludwig von Mises said:

> In any given moment the position of the individual ... in the society need not necessarily tie him down to one and the same activity. One man may be simultaneously landlord, wage-earner, and capitalist; another simultaneously entrepreneur, employee, and landlord; a third entrepreneur, capitalist, and landlord, etc. One may produce cheese and baskets and hire himself out occasionally as a day labourer. But even the situation of those who find themselves in approximately equal positions differs

according to the special circumstances in which they appear on the market. Even as a buyer for his own consumption every man is situated differently from others according to his special needs. On the market there are always only single individuals.[54]

If you think of yourself as a lifelong employee, it will become a self-fulfilling prophecy. As long as you see yourself as an employee, you will remain one. You don't have to be. In fact, you don't have to be only an employer or only an employee.

Many unjobbers develop multiple income streams in order to support themselves. They adopt many different ways of making money that are enjoyable. Such choices allow unjobbers to live a life that is congruent with their values. If you want to quit your job, you might have to find unconventional ways to support yourself. For example, you might find numerous ways of making a little money rather than one particular job that provides your entire income.

Most often, multiple income streams can begin as "side hustles" while supporting yourself from a regular job. This is how Michael Fogler described the transition to supporting yourself from a side hustle:

> The ideal is to completely combine how you spend your time on things that you really love to do with income earning, so that they go together 100 percent. In a perfect world, that would be great for everybody. Even if it can't be done 100 percent, it can be done to some percent; the higher, the better. I know a lot of people who don't like their job and want to be doing something else. A good way to do that is to see if you can, little by little, reduce the time that the job takes up, allowing more time for the other thing that you really like. And maybe, in time, you can find ways to bring in money with the activity that you love to do. And little by little those percentages can change. It may be a long process, but people feel better as long as they see that they are going in that

direction.[55]

Unjobbers and Taxes

Any attempt to lower expenses will be most effective if it addresses the biggest expenditures first. Taxes are typically the most significant household expense.

The frugal living approach that Michael Fogler and many other unjobbers adopt is a low-tax strategy. Income tax is progressive, so the more income you earn, the less efficient your earning is in terms of after-tax income. Michael minimizes his tax liability legally, because he runs his life on a low-income, low-expense model. He also actively seeks out ways to legally avoid taxation by responding to the tax code incentives. He learns all the legitimate deductions and utilizes them.

For Michael and many other unjobbers, minimizing taxes paid to the state is not only a practical matter of reducing expenses, but also a moral issue. Michael points out that government originally created the income tax in order to pay for the high cost of waging war:

> Most people do not realize that, were it not for wars and the preparations for wars, the income tax might not ever have been created. Wage earners, under the income tax, now needed to earn a much higher "gross" income in order to net what they were used to making prior to the income tax

Michael goes on to explain how his view of the ethics of taxation has informed his own approach to minimizing his tax liability:

> Noting all of the out-of-alignment (for me) expenditures that the federal government makes, I decided that this was another major reason to get out of the job-dominated life. With a home-based life centered around truly living and serving, and not centered around increasing my money intake, I am also not sending my money to the US government. I believe that there are simpler, more joyous, more truly democratic (people empowering), and more effective ways of creating our common good than by channeling our money through a large central government. ... I believe that I have the right to live according to my conscience, and that I have the right to freely exercise my conscientiously held beliefs as long as that exercise harms no one else. How could I, as a peace activist, work for peace and pray for peace, and then pay for war, environmental destruction, and corruption? I avoid paying federal income tax in ways that, even according to the IRS, are legal.[56]

Michael is making a moral argument as to why he aims to reduce his tax by every available means. Tax avoidance is integral to living according to his ethical code.

Things to Consider About Unjobbing

There are pros and cons to each strategy for job-free living. The main advantage of unjobbing is that you can achieve job freedom much faster than with other strategies. (For example, saving for financial independence takes many more years.) I see the goal of unjobbers—to only work on projects that give them fulfillment every day—as a positive vision for life.

The main disadvantage of unjobbing is that it does not provide financial independence. Unjobbers still have to work regularly in order to support themselves. If you love your work, then you might not consider this a problem because your "work" is an activity that you would do even if you didn't need the money. Nonetheless, unjobbing does not give you the flexibility and security that financial independence can bring.

You will have to decide how feasible it is to rely on unjobbing for your income. In their book *Your Money or Your Life*, Joe Dominguez and Vicki Robin provide a critique of the feasibility of an unjobbing approach to earning money:

> There is no guarantee that you will find someone to pay you to do what you feel called to do. It may take many years to develop your art or your research or your social innovation or your new technology to the point where those who have money want to pay for it. Most often this has less to do with the real value of your work than it has to do with luck, chance, perseverance, connections or a host of other factors. By giving up the expectation that you will be paid to do the work you are passionate about, you can do both things with more integrity. You can make money to cover your expenses, and you can follow your heart without compromise.

I imagine that unjobbing may be hard to sustain into old age. A young person might find it relatively easy to live a frugal life and support himself doing something fulfilling, even if it doesn't make him a huge amount of money. He might earn enough to support himself, but he may not be able to build up savings. It may be harder to sustain that kind of life if he has a family and his financial needs increase. It may also become unfeasible as he gets older, since he won't have passive income to fall back on.

Nonetheless, there are examples of people who have unjobbed for decades. Michael Fogler is happily unjobbing in his sixties and had no concerns when I spoke to him about it.

You just need to accept the consequences, especially that unjobbing will probably not provide financial independence.

Further Resources on Unjobbing

Podcast Episodes

Episode 34—Unjobbing: Author Interview with Michael Fogler[57]

Episode 118—Decluttering and Community Selling: Interview with Jorja Leavitt[58]

Episode 128—Be More Expansive Than Your Expertise: An Interview with Elliott Hulse[59]

Episode 171—From Million Dollar House to Tiny Home: Interview with Jacki Rigoni[60]

Books

The best introduction to unjobbing is Michael Fogler's original book, *Un-Jobbing*.[61] If you are interested in simple living and decluttering, Peter Walsh's book, *It's All Too Much*,[62] has lots of helpful suggestions. *You Have Too Much Shit,* by Chris Thomas, provides an humorous take on adopting voluntary simplicity. It is available for free online.[63]

CHAPTER THREE
Lifestyle Businesses

Can a business be used to change the world, like The Body Shop or Patagonia? Yes, but that isn't our goal here. Can a business be used to cash out through an IPO or sale? Yes, but that isn't our goal either. Our goal is simple: to create an automated vehicle for generating cash without consuming time.
—Tim Ferriss

Pat Flynn's Story

Pat Flynn worked in an architectural practice doing CAD drawings. When the great recession hit in 2008, his company downsized him out of a job. He hadn't planned to work for himself, but he needed to find a new way to make a living.

Around the time that he lost his job, Flynn had been studying for various technical certifications. He had kept a blog about the things he learned as he studied. Partly as a break from studying, he spent a lot of time improving the blog until it became a very professional website.

Without planning it, Flynn created a unique resource for people studying for the same exams as he was. The blog became very popular. Flynn added advertisements to the blog, which brought in a little income. Then he started selling e-books, which brought more income. Gradually he added a range of products to the website to bring in even more.

Flynn had moved from being an employee to being someone with an online business selling digital products. He now runs a website called *Smart Passive Income*,[64] through which he helps others develop similar businesses. You can read about his story in his book, *Let Go*.[65]

The Mindset Behind a Lifestyle Business

I'm using Flynn as an example of a *lifestyle business* that is used to fund a job-free life. As you read this chapter, bear in mind that this is just *one* way to run a business, and not the only way. Other kinds of business can give you a job-free life. We will explore more options afterwards.

Lifestyle entrepreneurs have a different motivation behind work to unjobbers. Whereas unjobbers want to spend time working on activities that they find fulfilling, a lifestyle business owner aims to spend as little time as possible working.

Lifestyle entrepreneurs view their businesses as a means to an end. They develop a business in order to make money efficiently. They want to maximize their time outside the business.

For example, someone who rents out properties is probably not doing so because she finds property rental fulfilling in itself. Rather, she aims to make money that will give her more freedom. She may also gain fulfillment from her mastery of the business challenges or from the professionalism that she exercises. Nonetheless, the business is more of a means to an end than a calling.

Creating a lifestyle business involves undertaking entrepreneurial risk. Someone developing a business usually invests their own resources and puts them at a greater risk—for the potential of greater reward—than the saver who uses passive investments. All entrepreneurship involves investing resources with an uncertain return and the possibility of loss.

The goal of this approach is to make as much money as possible with the minimum effort necessary. The purpose of a lifestyle business is to give you an income and a lot of free time, enabling you to find fulfillment outside the business.

Examples of Lifestyle Businesses

The 4-Hour Workweek[66] by Tim Ferriss was an influential book that encouraged people to start lifestyle businesses. Ferriss himself used a combination of a lifestyle business and selling a startup (more about that in Startups). However, his book provided a vision of a lifestyle supported by a business that only requires four hours of work per week. That vision has inspired many to try to replicate this approach.

Typically, a lifestyle business involves a lot of up-front work to create a recurring revenue stream, either from property or from products that you can scale very easily.

One of the most common lifestyle businesses is based on the ownership and rental of real estate. Rosie Tran is a comedian and host of *Out Of The Box*[67] podcast. She is working towards financial independence together with her husband. Rosie described to me how she witnessed success with the real estate lifestyle business strategy within her family:

> My uncle is an immigrant. He barely speaks any English, but after starting on $20,000 a year as a city worker, he is now a multimillionaire with over 100 rental properties. He and my aunt were both working, and they used one income to support themselves while they poured the other income into investing in foreclosed properties that they fixed up. Once you have two, three, or four properties, it turns into a giant snowball of passive income.[68]

Real estate is not the only kind of business that can provide passive income. In recent years, it has been increasingly possible to create online businesses that provide similar benefits. The idea is to create a digital product that you can resell many times online.

An e-book is an example of a digital product that can provide passive income. Companies like Amazon have opened up publishing to the masses, removing barriers to entry in this business. Traditional publishing companies used to act as gatekeepers, which meant that you could only publish your books if you managed to persuade a publisher that the risk was worth it. Now, with the Internet, you can take on the risk yourself and see if you can find a market.

Todd Tresidder is a self-made millionaire who now runs the website *Financial Mentor*,[69] teaching others how to develop their wealth. When I interviewed Todd, he described how he developed online products on the back of his mentoring work:

> A common issue that I deal with is how much money you need to retire. I run into that with virtually every client, since they are all in pursuit of financial freedom. After a while, I got down a system, so I wrote a book called How Much Money Do I Need To Retire? [70] Last time I checked, it was actually number one for the keywords "retirement planning." It took a lot of work to produce a really good book. But that book is sitting up there and it's selling around 400 copies a month, so I am building a relationship with 400 or so people a month. I sat down for a period of time, worked hard, got it down, and now it just multiplies.[71]

You can also transform a more traditional offline business into a lifestyle business model. David Kahn is an entrepreneur who listens to my podcast. He contacted me from Chiang Mai, Thailand, to tell me about his experience in transforming his business to enable him and his family to travel the world. David described his business transformation:

> I started a business that solves complex problems for our clients using a suite of enterprise resource planning products that Microsoft manufactures. ... Every single thing that I did in the business, I always asked myself, "Am I doing this in a way that is going to free me from being able to do it in the future?" That means building processes, training, documentation, technology, and workflow, so that after I'm done doing it the first time, everything is ready for others to do it in future.[72]

David created a lifestyle business based on consultancy services, not online information products. He manages his business over the Internet, even though the work itself is still face-to-face and locally delivered.

Lifestyle Entrepreneurs and Taxes

Entrepreneurs use the advantages of running a business to

control their level of tax liability, much more than employees are able to. Joshua Sheats, the financial advisor and host of the *Radical Personal Finance*[73] podcast, described the difference in options available to employees and entrepreneurs when it comes to taxes:

> Individual employees have almost no flexibility with their tax planning. But the employer— the entrepreneur—even at the smallest level, has an incredible amount of flexibility. I was working with a couple recently who are both high-income employees. One spouse is a pharmacist and the other is a physical therapist. They said to me, "We pay so much in tax, what can we do?" Unfortunately, as an employee there are a few little tricks, but none of them make nearly as big a difference as you could get if one of the spouses stopped working as a pharmacist and started running a pharmacy of their own instead. That would make a huge difference[74].

Here is how financial mentor Todd Tresidder described the entrepreneurial outlook in regard to taxes:

> The government has decided that they want to incentivize certain behavior, so they offer tax advantages to those behaviors in order to encourage activity there. ... Business entrepreneurship is an example: a tremendous amount of expenses are deductible legitimately through a business as an entrepreneur. There are all kinds of tax advantages built into the code by design. It behooves you to learn that and it puts money in your pocket every year when you understand the tax law and you respond to it and create a smart strategy based on it.[75]

Location Independence

A lifestyle business gives you a lot of freedom as a business owner. For example, you don't need to be located in the same country as your business. You can take advantage of this freedom as an opportunity to minimize your expenses in many ways. One technique commonly used by lifestyle business owners for minimizing their expenses is *geo-arbitrage*. This means locating yourself somewhere with low-cost living expenses and selling your digital products through the Internet to markets that can afford to pay well.

Pete Sisco is a self-made millionaire who enjoys a lifestyle of perpetual travel with his wife. He was one of the pioneers of using self-publishing on the Internet, starting back in the 1990s. Here is how Pete described his lifestyle of perpetual travel to me:

> Around 2005, I had been earning my income online and only online for several years. Gradually, it began to dawn on me that because all my income came from online sources, I really had the ability to live anywhere that I wanted. At the time, I was living in the United States. I first said to myself, "Why am I living in a state that has state income tax? I should move to one of the states that has no state income tax." Gradually, in that process, I thought, "Why am I even living in a country with federal income tax?" That doesn't work for everybody—I happen to not be an American. (It's very difficult for Americans to escape their domestic taxes.) So I started to look at the whole world as a place that I could live.
>
> Ever since early 2006 my wife and I have traveled. At that time, some of our kids were still younger and we all traveled together. We started in Belize and Mexico—two countries that I really like. I lived in Belize long enough to become a permanent resident. That was a tactical move because Belize is a tax haven country. (If you are a resident of Belize, they do not tax any income that you earn outside Belize.) Since then, we've lived in Thailand, mainland China, the UK, Crete, and Malaysia.
>
> It's a very liberating lifestyle. I've turned into a real evangelist for it. I am such a believer in the freedom that it gives you. It's unlike anything that human beings have experienced for centuries—other than people who were born into fantastically wealthy families. For the average person who has to earn income and has

bills to pay every month, it's almost unimaginably liberating to make income from an Internet business that does not require you to live in any one place.[76]

Delegation and Outsourcing

A business will only give you free time if you don't have to manage it every day, so lifestyle entrepreneurs tend to use as many techniques for delegation as possible. The idea is to delegate as much of your own tasks in running the business as you can.

One way to do this is to hire virtual assistants. These people work for you online to do any tasks that don't require your own efforts. As virtual assistants tend to be located in low-cost countries, this technique is also another example of minimizing expenses through geo-arbitrage.

It is possible to benefit from outsourcing many functions, beyond assistant roles. David Kahn told me about how he uses outsourcing to keep his consultancy business as lean as possible, giving him less to manage:

> A client can show up anywhere in the country and occasionally anywhere in the world. As soon as that client expresses a need, we try to meet that unique need geographically, functionally, product-module-wise, language-wise, etc., by working with a large community of independent consultants around the world. We've established a network of resources that specialize in different areas. We even call on our competitors for resources. We cherry-pick from those resources to bring together the most relevant team that is physically present for the client.
> When you look at what traditional companies do, they put the person who is on the bench—who is not engaged at another project—on your project, regardless of whether or not that person has the right skill set. We don't have people sitting on the bench. Instead, we look for that right person for your project—a person who is in your area. So our customers give us the feedback that

they get a much more relevant team than they've had with competitors.

You pay a little bit more [to run your business in this way] because you are typically using more experienced people who can charge you higher bill rates or because you're paying a competitor, so there's overhead in that. So you take a little less profit there, but on the flip side you save enough in overhead costs for not having them on the payroll (and in your benefits and so on) and from not having any underutilization costs where they're not engaged and you are still paying their salary.[77]

Here's how Pete Sisco described his use of worldwide outsourcing to create his e-books:

> There's a fellow in New Zealand who I have never met in person, but I have done business with for over ten years. He created all my e-book covers. I really love the fact that he and I can transact business on a value-for-value basis and there are no third parties that step into the picture. ... There is no international ministry of e-book publication and distribution that makes a whole bunch of rules about minimum prices—who knows what regulation they could come up with. All that just gets stripped away. Two people can do trade with each other from literally halfway around the world, and there's never been a hiccup. That is the future of the world.[78]

Things to Consider About Lifestyle Businesses

If you like the idea of a lifestyle business, it is important to consider how you feel about running a company aside from the potential benefit of more free time that it might give you.

Only a small fraction of entrepreneurs manage to arrange their businesses in such a way to truly deliver the kind of lifestyle freedom described in this chapter. There is no guarantee that you will be able to run a business on just a few hours of work a week. You may miscalculate the potential and find that your business requires all your time to stay afloat.

Many entrepreneurs imagine that their business will deliver passive income, when the reality is more often that it could deliver recurring income, which is very different. Recurring income is simply income that you receive on an ongoing basis, rather than a one-time payment. It is tempting to think of this income as "passive," since the money keeps coming in. But how much ongoing work do you need to do to keep that recurring income flowing? If you have to work on your business all day, it is not providing *passive* income; it is just giving you *recurring* income.

I share the enthusiasm that lifestyle entrepreneurs have for finding ways to extract themselves from the day-to-day operations of their businesses. It is healthy for your own sanity not to be stuck firefighting in the business. It's better for the health of the business if it is not dependent on the entrepreneur's constant tinkering to survive.

It is also good for your humility to ensure that the business doesn't revolve around you. The mission of a business is to help customers, not to make the entrepreneur feel wanted or look important.

Building a business requires a huge investment of effort. Even if you eventually create a business that will give you a lot of free time, it will still require a lot of work to get started. To be a successful business owner, you need the stamina to keep building your venture in the face of significant challenges.

If your motivation for starting a business is purely "to

create an automated vehicle for generating cash without consuming time," as Tim Ferriss put it, then it will be a failure if it does consume your time. However, if you build a business to achieve a goal that you feel passionate about, then it may not matter so much if you spend more of your time working than you initially hoped.

Motivation in entrepreneurship is a matter of personal choice. I created a business because I believed in the purpose—it was in line with my vision for how I could improve the lives of others.[79] Part of the fun of entrepreneurship is the chance to bring something into the world that reflects your values. I view entrepreneurship as an opportunity to express character.

If you find a way to gain fulfillment from *doing* business (rather than solely from the free time that your business income gives you) then it doesn't matter if you end up spending more hours working. You are still going to be your own boss. You will still have a job-free life.

Further Resources on Lifestyle Businesses

Podcast Episodes

Episode 119—How To Develop Your Wealth Plan: An Interview With Todd Tressider[80]

Episode 130— Perpetual Travelers Part 2: Interview With Pete Sisco[81]

Episode 131— Perpetual Travelers Part 3: Interview with David Kahn[82]

Episode 147— Out Of The Box Interview: Financial

Freedom and Personal Development[83]

Episode 209—Tax Strategies And Financial Freedom Part 1 (Interview With Joshua Sheats)[84]

Books

If you are interested in reading about lifestyle businesses, I recommend you start with *The 4-Hour Workweek* by Tim Ferriss[85] to get an overview of this approach to entrepreneurship. You may also enjoy Pat Flynn's short book, *Let Go,*[86] for a personal story of his journey into this kind of business.

Some entrepreneurship books are useful for both lifestyle businesses and startups. Michael Gerber's classic, *The E-Myth Revisited*[87] is a great guide for how to make a business scalable. *Rework,*[88] by Jason Fried and David Heinemeier Hansson, is a more up-to-date guide to best practices.

Harry Browne's book, *How I Found Freedom in an Unfree World,*[89] is more personal and broader in scope, but it has a strong focus on entrepreneurship and is an all-round inspiring read. Although the focus is on startups, I cover topics relevant to all entrepreneurship in my own book, *Becoming An Entrepreneur.*[90]

CHAPTER FOUR
Startups

If you want a happy ending, that depends, of course, on where you stop your story.
—Orson Welles

Derek Sivers's Story

Derek Sivers was a musician and circus clown. He wanted to sell his music as an independent musician, so he made a website called *CD Baby*[91] to sell his CDs. Before long, other independent musicians came to him and asked if he would sell their CDs through his website too. CD Baby grew to become the largest online independent music store in the world.

Derek sold his business in 2008 for over $20 million. All the proceeds from the sale went into a charitable trust that he created, which gives him a five percent drawdown each year, for the rest of his life. Upon his death, the trust will be used to support independent musicians. While he is alive, it provides him with an income.

Derek now writes about entrepreneurship and has

started various other businesses and fun projects that have meaning for him. His book, *Anything You Want*[92], describes the growth and sale of his business. He also has a blog, sivers.org, where you can find out more about his approach to life.

Startups as a Route to Job Freedom

You can milk a business for income, but you can also build its capital value through growth. Ideally, you want to do both, but there is a trade-off between taking income and building the value of the business. If you had to focus, which would be your priority?

If you prioritize getting income to support your preferred lifestyle, then you are building a lifestyle business (as discussed in the previous chapter).

If you choose to focus on building the value of your business, rather than milking it, then your model is a startup. The challenge of building a startup can provide a fulfilling job-free lifestyle. There is also a financial goal at the end of this challenge: the value of the business itself can ultimately provide you with the wealth to live from. If you succeed in selling your business for enough money, then you can live job-free from your investments.

Although startups have a different focus to lifestyle businesses, a business can evolve from either one into the other. For example, a business can start out providing a lifestyle, but evolve into a growth startup.

Some people might prefer to own a lifestyle business for decades, whereas others might aim to sell a startup as quickly as possible. I've chosen to cover these two approaches to entrepreneurship separately because it is possible to focus exclusively on either approach.

Is selling the business an integral part of a startup entrepreneur's plan? Some entrepreneurs argue, on the contrary, that if you want to start a business, you should do it without any intention to sell.[93]

As a business owner, you have a job-free life—you work for yourself. If you love working on your business, you may not want to sell, because you are already doing what you most enjoy every day. However, it is possible to love your business and yet still aim to sell it one day. I loved running my pedestrian movement consulting business. Nonetheless, my aim from the beginning was to sell it when I could.

One of my motivations for becoming an entrepreneur was that I wanted financial freedom. I wanted to do many things with my life, not just run one particular business. I saw the business as a major life project. I knew it was a commitment that would last for many years. But I also wanted to do something else afterward. Now that I have sold my business, I am writing, podcasting, and traveling the world.

Whatever your motivations, you will leave the business one day, one way or another. Nobody lives forever. Something is going to happen to your business when you are no longer able to exercise the responsibilities of owning it. Unless you go out of business involuntarily before then, there are only two ultimate fates for your company. Either your business will close down, or it will carry on without you.

If your business has value, then winding it down would be a senseless destruction of that value. But in order for the business to continue, somebody has to exercise the responsibilities of an owner. For that to happen, you have to successfully transfer ownership to someone else.

I suggest every entrepreneur give due consideration to how they might sell in future. Like all things, your involvement in the business must end someday. Selling gives you the most positive ending.

Homeowners are careful to maintain and upgrade their homes, in awareness of future sale value. Similarly, having an eye towards a future business sale provides a great incentive for you—as an entrepreneur—to maintain and upgrade your business. It incentivizes you to make the business as valuable as possible and to minimize its dependence on you. It encourages you to implement the systems necessary to allow your operation to run without you.

Best of all, you will create the conditions necessary so that one day, if you do it right, your business may give you the opportunity to quit the rat race. It will give you financial independence, which is a launch pad to do whatever you want with your life. What a great way to end your involvement in the business.

How Building and Selling a Startup Works

The strategy for achieving financial independence by

building and selling a startup can be summarized in five points:

1. Start a scalable business (one that is capable of significant growth).
2. Grow the business to the size and profitability level that makes it sellable.
3. Find a buyer.
4. Negotiate a sale.
5. Invest the proceeds from your sale and live from your investments.

Making a Scalable Business

In his book, *Built to Sell*,[94] John Warrillow emphasizes the importance of specialization as a key to making a business scalable, which in turn will make it sellable. He recommends turning down unique or customized projects that do not contribute to the advancement of your standardized operation, even if you were previously dependent on such work for a large part of your revenue. If you want to sell your business, you have to stop doing generalist work. Instead, you must focus exclusively on work that is truly scalable, repeatable, and productized.

How do you make your operation scalable? In *The E-Myth Revisited*,[95] Michael Gerber put forward the idea that you should design your business as if it were a franchise prototype. Even if you never intend to set up a franchise chain, by designing your own business as if it were a franchise prototype, you create the procedures necessary for the business to run itself effectively and to allow for growth.

Gerber recommends creating an operations manual that details procedures for specific tasks and designates clear responsibilities.

Gerber's approach is about getting you, the entrepreneur, out of the day-to-day operations of the business so that the business can grow without you being a bottleneck. He describes this as working *on* your business rather than *in* your business.

In *Becoming an Entrepreneur*,[96] I describe my experience with extracting myself from operations in a chapter called "Make Yourself Redundant". The ongoing, iterative approach I suggest is threefold:

- Standardize your product or service, so you are not reinventing the wheel each time you fulfill an order for a customer.
- Proceduralize your operations, so that all workflows are well-defined and can be easily repeated and controlled for quality.
- Optimize your procedures, using mechanization and automation to make them as efficient as you can.

Growth and Profitability

In almost all cases, selling is only viable if your business is both large enough and sufficiently profitable. Many small business owners want to sell their businesses before they have reached the right size or level of profitability. They just want to give up, get out of the business, and get paid. That is not a compelling sales proposition. Let's address the issues of size and profitability in turn.

Regarding size, your business must generate enough revenue to make buying it worthwhile for an acquirer. Most potential acquirers will not even look at your business if the revenue is too small. Below a certain level, no deal is worth the transaction cost to them. The legal and administrative costs of buying a business are more or less the same for a company worth a few hundred thousand dollars as they are for a company worth a few million. It is much easier to buy a bigger business because the transaction costs become a negligible fraction of the deal, whereas the deal costs alone can make buying a very small company unprofitable.

I received this message myself when speaking to some potential buyers during the earlier stages of my business. Although they were interested in purchasing our consultancy, they had a minimum-revenue threshold. As a matter of policy, they didn't consider any acquisitions below that threshold.

There are always exceptional cases—companies with no revenue that sell for millions because they seem to promise great potential in the future. It is also possible to sell small companies, but often only for a price that will not give you the kind of payout needed for financial independence. In my opinion, any company with a revenue below about $3 million per year is going to be hard to sell, owing to its small size.

As well as size, your business must also generate a high profit margin in order to be sellable. Again, there are exceptions—some Internet startups sell for good money without ever having made a profit, but these are extremely unusual. The vast majority of business purchasers want to buy an income stream based on demonstrated profits.

If you explore potential sales opportunities for your startup at a time when you are making good profits, you will have options for where to take the business: you can either sell, or simply keep earning good money. You will have a strong negotiating position. I was not in any hurry to sell, because I had a profitable business. I was able to walk away from negotiations until the terms were good enough.

Finding a Buyer

There are many ways to sell ownership, such as a trade sale, floating your business on the stock exchange, or selling to your employees in a management buyout. I sold my business through a trade sale, which is the most common route to selling a business. It is also the easiest way to sell, in my opinion. My comments in this chapter will focus on this route.

The company acquiring your business needs to be big enough to be able to afford the purchase. If an acquirer has less than five times your revenue, buying your business becomes a bet-the-company decision. Should the acquisition fail to deliver on its promise, it would probably kill the acquiring company. No one will want to buy your business under those conditions.

On the other hand, if a buyer's business is significantly bigger than yours, then purchasing your business might not make any appreciable difference to their financial performance. In such a case, it might not be worth the effort of undertaking the purchase. Warrillow has suggested a "5 to 20 rule" for acquisitions: the purchasing company tends to be between 5 and 20 times the size of the business that they are acquiring.[97]

You may be able to sell to a much bigger company if your business has a particular strategic value to a specific buyer. My business provided pedestrian movement simulation and analysis. The multinational engineering consultancy purchased us because they could utilize our specialist expertise on a great number of projects. Purchasing the business did virtually nothing for their end-of-year accounts because we were so tiny compared to them. Nonetheless, the acquisition gave them enough of a strategic advantage for the future to make the purchase worthwhile. They saw opportunities to add our services to many of the much larger projects that they were undertaking, thereby adding significant value to the client and improving their competitive position.

Try to find a buyer who wants your business for more than just the impact that you will have on this year's financial statement. A strategic advantage of some kind is where the real value lies.

It is important to develop relationships with potential buyers before you consider selling. I was able to sell my business because we had developed strong partnering relationships with many other companies that could potentially have been buyers of our business. Every time you work together with a bigger company in the same field, you are dealing with a potential buyer.

If you develop good working relationships, then you build

trust, and potential buyers get to see the value you provide. That helps the negotiation because you are not starting from zero. You've already got something very valuable that the other party in the negotiation knows about.

Buying a company is a difficult task that is fraught with risk. If you want someone to buy your business, make the decision easier for them by earning their trust. An effective way to do this is developing a working relationship with your potential buyer long before any discussion of a sale.

Working together achieves two things. Firstly, it highlights the value of your offer because the acquiring company can see your business in action. Secondly, it gives you a platform to earn their trust by exhibiting your dependability in real working situations.

As a specialist consultancy, we were often subcontracted by the big engineering company that eventually bought our business. They would add us into their projects to provide specialist expertise. Over a long period, we demonstrated that we added value to their projects. We developed a relationship of trust long before the sale.

You may be able to develop partnering relationships with bigger, complimentary companies that might be potential acquirers. Partnering and affiliate relationships can help grow your business. They are also great ways to find potential acquirers.

Like any type of sale, the sale of a business doesn't just happen; it requires planning and work. It requires you to understand the buyer's needs. You, as the seller, have to do the selling. You have to develop the value proposition. I spent over a year working on removing barriers to the sale of my business, on top of all the years spent growing it and making it more profitable.

Negotiating a Sale

When you sell a business, you exchange your ownership for a multiple of expected future annual profit.[98] The multiple used to determine the sale price depends very much on negotiation and varies from industry to industry. It comes down to how much profit you make and what multiple of that profit the buyer is willing to give you to get ownership of the business.

So many issues can go wrong in a sale negotiation that I strongly recommend paying for a good advisor if you intend to sell. There are warranties, guarantees, and insurance liabilities to consider. Will the acquiring company pay you in cash or in shares? Will some part of your payment depend on specific performance targets? What proportion of the total sum?

I could have made big mistakes about all these important issues if I had not had good advice. We found an excellent advisor who had negotiated many previous business sales. He knew all the issues that tend to come up, so he was able to help us make informed decisions.

A buyer will usually require you to stay on in the business for a period after the sale to help reach certain performance targets and ensure that the business keeps making money as it is supposed to. This "earn-out" period usually lasts a couple of years. I stayed on for three years after the sale of my business.

Another aspect of the earn-out is how much of the money is going to be dependent on the performance of the business after the sale. In short, the buyer may want to set performance targets that you must meet following the sale, in order to trigger the release of some fraction of the money. These are the kinds of issues that you need a good advisor to help you with during the negotiation.

Living from Investments

Like extreme savers, startup entrepreneurs aim for financial independence. However, their strategy for achieving it is different. Most extreme savers are employees who save the majority of their paycheck and gradually build up an investment portfolio over a period of about ten years. They get incrementally closer to the point at which they can retire and live from their investment income.

In contrast, entrepreneurs often deplete their personal savings to fund themselves during the startup phase, but those who sell their businesses get a big payout eventually. The process of growing your startup into a valuable asset is usually long and slow. However, when you sell the business, you realize the value of that asset all at once. If you sell for a sufficient price, it will put you in a similar position to the extreme savers: you will be able to live from your investments.

Selling a startup is like extreme saving compressed into one payout. If you get a good enough price, you can invest the vast majority of your payout and live from the returns indefinitely. This can facilitate a *zero-hour* workweek, whereby you live from truly passive investments.

Entrepreneurs who sell their startups can pole-vault their way to financial independence, by gaining a big lump sum upon exit, rather than by accumulating savings over a long period, as the intensive savers do. Successful entrepreneurs can get bigger payouts to retire from than extreme savers because a business has more growth potential than a salary income. On the other hand, most businesses never reach the point of a successful exit for the founder.

I used all my personal savings and took out large debts to fund myself and my business during the first two years after startup. I then worked for seven years building the business and reaching profitability. My route to financial independence was the payout I received from selling the business.

After the sale and the earn-out period, startup entrepreneurs follow the same path as the intensive savers. You achieve financial independence when you have enough money saved that you can live from your investments sustainably. (See more details about this in Appendix A: About Investing). If you can withdraw a safe amount each year from passive investments, then you can do whatever you want with your time. Some people choose to start more businesses, as Derek Sivers did. The point is to have the freedom to do whatever you want.

Things to Consider About Startups

If you are interested in building a startup, I suggest you

consider how you will feel if you are never able to sell it. Very few businesses reach the size and profitability required for a successful exit. Financial independence is a great goal to aim for, but if you are *only* interested in your company as a vehicle to eventually sell, you probably won't enjoy a startup entrepreneur's life.

Even if you make it to profitability, you may not be able to sell for years. The business cycle has a big effect on the willingness of companies to consider acquisitions. If the timing is bad, you may find it hard to find a buyer through no fault of your own. You may have to wait years until the broader economic conditions are favorable again.

I was very lucky with the timing of my sale. I sold in 2007, during a time of relative economic optimism. The market for company acquisitions was much better before the crash of 2008 than afterwards. Such macro-economic factors are outside your control.

If you enjoy the adventure of entrepreneurship in itself, then it doesn't matter so much if you don't find a way to sell. Building a startup is already a job-free lifestyle. You get to be your own boss and spend every day working on the project that is most meaningful to you. If you can gain fulfillment from the startup lifestyle itself, then it is not the end of the world if you don't manage to sell.

Even if you do have an opportunity to sell, it has downsides that are worth considering. Selling my business was one of the high points in my life so far, but it was also bittersweet. You cannot grow a business to profitability without pouring your heart and soul into it. What kept me going was my belief in the venture. I knew that we were doing great work. I felt a painful sense of loss when it was time to let go of my business.

There is often a gulf between what the buyers of a business are buying and what the seller thinks they are selling. As a seller, you have spent years developing a company culture. Your procedures are not only the way that you do business, they are also the source of your efficiency and they represent your way of working. I viewed my company culture as extremely valuable.

However, buyers have different priorities. Many buyers are not interested in buying a different company culture—they already have their own way of working that took years to develop. They are often most interested in purchasing the resources of a business to add to their own. In my case, the resources within my business were the software that we created and the people undertaking the analysis.

I sold my business to a very large multinational consultancy that wanted my business to conform to their procedures. We had to move to their premises, use their IT systems, and become fully assimilated into their working culture.

It was painful to watch them throw away all the hard-won methods of working that I had developed for my company. I found it hard to see the new owners making decisions about my business that I would not have made. Part of selling a business is coming to terms with the sense of loss.

Further Resources on Startups

Podcast Episodes

Episode 53—Entrepreneurship Part 8: Selling Your Business[99]

Episode 107—What Kind of Business Should I Start?[100]

Episode 121—The Big Decisions for Entrepreneurs[101]

Episode 161—Review of *Built to Sell* by John Warrillow[102]

Episode 207—Who Will Buy Your Business?[103]

Books

My book, *Becoming an Entrepreneur*,[104] provides an overview of the process of building a startup and is a good place to start. *The Lean Startup*, by Eric Ries,[105] is a helpful manual for startup entrepreneurs covering more technical details. *The Art of The Start*, by Guy Kawasaki,[106] is also good as a general introduction. Derek Sivers's book, *Anything You Want*, is a fascinating account of the process of selling a business.[107]

There are two key books on the process of selling. *Built To Sell,* by John Warrillow,[108] is a useful how-to guide for the whole process of building and selling a startup. *Finish Big,* by Bo Burlingam, has many interviews with entrepreneurs who sold, and contains a more detailed discussion of technical topics such as valuation.[109]

Three general entrepreneurship books that I previously mentioned for lifestyle businesses are also relevant for startups—*The E-Myth Revisited*[110] *by* Michael Gerber, *Rework,*[111] by Jason Fried and David Heinemeier Hansson, and Harry Browne's book, *How I Found Freedom in an Unfree World*.[112]

See also Appendix A: About Investing for more resources on the investment side of selling a startup as a route to financial independence.

CHAPTER FIVE

Choosing a Job-Free Lifestyle

There is only one success—to be able to spend your life in your own way.
—Christopher Morley

Nobody learns how to live a job-free life in school or college. We are all taught to be employees. Nobody shows you how to take advantage of all the opportunities for creating a lifestyle where you don't *need* a job. The focus of the entire education system is employee conditioning. Having a job is the default lifestyle.

There is nothing inherently wrong with having a job. Periods of employment can even serve an important role in the process of achieving a job-free lifestyle. The problem is that many people would rather live a life free of jobs, but they don't know how to make that dream a reality.

You have now read about four different strategies for living job free, with real-world examples for each. You've learned about people who achieved financial independence and early retirement. You've seen others who make a living without a job, as unjobbers or entrepreneurs.

Which of these lifestyles would work for you? There is no single answer for everyone, as it is a matter of personal choice. In this chapter, I lay out some of the considerations that you can use to decide which of these different job-free lifestyles may be right for you, and in what stage of your life they may be relevant.

Key Questions to Consider

Here are some questions to ask yourself to help you choose from different strategies for quitting the rat race and becoming job free:

How frugally are you willing to live? Some strategies for achieving a job-free life involve extreme saving and living very frugally for many years. Think about the changes to your spending patterns required to save intensively. Would you be happy with that lifestyle?

How long are you willing to wait? If you plan to achieve job freedom through extreme saving, you should reckon with spending around ten years as an employee first, during your accumulation phase. Other strategies have the advantage that they enable you to quit your job much sooner, but they have their own downsides, as we will discuss.

How important is it for you to be your own boss? Many opportunities for living a job-free life come through entrepreneurship. For some people, their primary motivation is to be their own boss. But others just don't want to be entrepreneurs. They don't want the lifestyle or responsibilities of a business owner.

What is your level of risk tolerance? Entrepreneurship is a potentially high-reward choice, but also a high-risk one. How tolerant are you of the idea of potential failure? There is more risk involved in taking the entrepreneurial paths.

How marketable are your expertise and connections? The more skilled you are and the better connections you have, the more options will be open to you for living job free. Your choices will be limited if you're at a stage in life when you don't have valuable skills or good connections.

When to Choose Extreme Saving

Extreme saving is a good path to job freedom if you have a low tolerance for risk. You can use a steady job (or a stream of jobs) to get you to a point of early retirement and financial independence without risking your own venture. You don't have to be an entrepreneur.

If you become an extreme saver, you may need to be comfortable with a lifestyle of frugal living for the rest of your life. There are limits to the amount of money you can accumulate saving as an employee, so this strategy has less of a potential upside when compared to entrepreneurship.

You will benefit most from extreme saving if you are a highly skilled employee who prefers to work for someone else, rather than run a business. If you have highly marketable job skills, you can command a high salary and be relatively secure that you will always find a job. As long as you are willing to save the majority of your earnings, and as long as you don't mind working for someone else for ten years, this path to job-free living could work well for you.

There are also periods in life when extreme saving could be a great strategy—even if you later choose a different path to job freedom. For example, if you don't yet have valuable skills, good connections, or industry knowledge, then you are probably not well placed to start a business. Under these conditions, being an employee and pursuing a strategy of extreme saving could be a useful way to save the money that will give you options in the future.

Similarly, if you are in debt, then it makes sense to get a job and pursue extreme saving as a strategy to pay down your debt as quickly as possible. Debt is not a sound basis for starting an entrepreneurial venture. You can use extreme saving as an employee to pay down the debt. Once you are debt free, you can continue using extreme saving to accumulate the capital that will enable you to explore more entrepreneurial lifestyle choices.

Extreme saving is the best choice for people who want a low-risk plan for living job-free. There are many reasons why you might want a low-risk option. If you have kids or other dependents, then you may not want to risk the volatile income associated with starting a business. You may prefer the lower-risk, lower-reward, more secure option of extreme saving.

When to Choose Unjobbing

Unjobbing has the upside that it allows you to start living a job-free lifestyle with minimal delay. If you become a freelancer or live from multiple side hustles, you may be able to quit your job very quickly. I think unjobbing is a good option if you already have highly marketable skills or good connections within an industry.

The most successful unjobbers are those who use marketable skills to command good pay without the hassle of holding a job. Andrew, a good friend of mine, worked for many years as a management consultant. That industry has a culture of long hours and high-stress working. Andrew loved the work itself, but he became fed up with the high-pressure and long hours that went with it.

Andrew was able to quit his job and find work as a freelancer because he had an excellent reputation within the industry. He earned more by working one day a week as a freelancer than he had earned working long weeks of overtime as an employee.

As an unjobbing freelancer, Andrew would work intensively on a project for a week or so, and then take a month off. His job-free lifestyle enabled him to be a stay-at-home dad for much of the first couple of years of his son's life, undertaking the occasional work project to support his family. The unjobbing lifestyle worked well for Andrew because he had good connections, marketable skills, and a reliable source of clients.

Another friend of mine named Kyle built an unjobbing lifestyle for himself by becoming a freelance programmer. He was able to do short projects where he earned a lot of money and then take time off to travel.

The unjobbing life worked for Kyle because he had highly demanded skills. If you have good connections and significant skills, you may have the opportunity to become a freelancer and earn more than you would as a full-time employee.

Unjobbing is riskier than being a full-time employee, because you're taking on the responsibility of finding regular income. It is still less risky than starting a business because you usually have low overheads. Unjobbing requires little equipment—perhaps a laptop or something—and, therefore, little capital cost.

If you find after six months that you are not getting enough work as a freelancer, you can find another job. Your losses will be less than if you were pursuing one of the entrepreneurial routes to job freedom.

When to Choose a Lifestyle Business

Lifestyle entrepreneurship is for those who want to work for themselves and aim to use entrepreneurship as a vehicle to provide maximum free time. I think this choice works best for people who don't want to sell their business; they just want an ongoing source of income to support their freedom-oriented lifestyle.

You do need a greater tolerance for risk as a lifestyle business owner than as an extreme saver or unjobber, because you may have to invest money in developing your product or service. It may take longer before you start making enough money to support yourself. For these reasons, there is more at stake for you as a business owner than if you remain an employee or become a freelancer.

A lifestyle business may suit you if you want to be an entrepreneur and you don't want accountability to others. If you want to be able to do whatever you choose with your business and organize it entirely for your convenience, then a lifestyle business is probably the way to go.

If you prefer not to answer to anyone, you may be better oriented to a lifestyle business than a startup. This kind of business is suitable if you don't want to build a team or create a company culture, both of which involve accountability. Because many lifestyle entrepreneurs don't want the hassle of accountability to others, they are often solopreneurs—small businesses centered around one person.

Of course, any lifestyle business will only succeed if it provides value to customers and improves their lives. If you don't create something that people want, then your business won't sell anything. However, the main point of a lifestyle business is to give you freedom.

Because it is your venture, you will have maximum flexibility to organize it in any way you want. If there is potential for growth, but you don't particularly want to work harder and you're happy with the amount of income that you are earning, then you don't have to grow the business. If you can support yourself only working on the business one day per week, and you don't care about earning more, that's fine. It is your business; you can do whatever you want with it.

When to Choose Startup Entrepreneurship

Become a startup entrepreneur if you want to build a kick-ass company to pursue a purpose. With this option, your aim is to make an impact on the world through your business. Do you feel excited by the idea of creating an extraordinary organization that can have an impact on the world?

Startup entrepreneurs want to create a venture that has a life of its own. Typically, startups are larger ventures than lifestyle businesses. Startups involve building a team and creating a company culture. Create a startup if you are serious about building a company that's bigger than you and that can last longer.

This path involves the highest risk among the job-free lifestyles, but it also offers the potential for the highest rewards. As a startup entrepreneur, you build value in the company that you may be able to sell one day. It may suit you if you are interested in creating something lasting that you can sell, and then move on to other projects in life. It can give you financial independence and enable early retirement.

You need a high risk-tolerance though, because as well as having the highest potential upside, it also has the highest risk, since you are investing more of your money and effort into something that ultimately might not work.

If you run a startup, you are far more accountable to others than a lifestyle entrepreneur is. If you take funding, then you will be accountable to investors. If you want to build a successful team, you will have responsibilities toward your employees.

You will enjoy the startup lifestyle if you enjoy intense projects. Startups only seem to have one speed: maximum. If you like the idea of immersing yourself in the adventure of building a business, then this is the way to go. If you prefer to limit your involvement, then you may prefer a lifestyle business.

If you burn with the ambition to build a startup, I suggest it would be easier to launch your venture before you take on other major responsibilities, such as children. The beginning phase of any business is very intense, and will be far easier if you are not caring for dependents.

Moving Between Lifestyles

You can move between job-free lifestyles. This choice does not have to be for life. For example, Kyle—the programmer friend I mentioned—made the transition between three of the job-free lifestyle strategies.

Kyle started unjobbing as a freelance developer. Eventually, he developed a couple of applications of his own that he sold online. His apps became a lifestyle business, which provided him with reasonable income and lots of free time. Then he decided one of his apps could become the basis of a bigger commercial venture. He is now building a startup that aims to serve a huge potential market.

Whichever path to job freedom you choose, it doesn't have to be a lifetime commitment. You can change course later. For example, you can be an extreme saver all the way to early retirement, or you can change course along the way and use some of your savings to start a business if you want.

If You Are Unsure About What to Do

If you want a job-free life but you are not sure which path to pursue, I suggest you consider extreme saving as the default starting point on your journey. Extreme saving requires the least risk and the least imagination. It is the simplest strategy to follow.

Saving is also a very good strategy to start with if you're straight out of school or college and you don't have a lot of skills or contacts. As you work a job and save money, you can use your time in employment to gain the skills and contacts that you will need for other ventures. Extreme saving will enable you to build up resources that can give you the leeway to try other job-free adventures.

In the end, your freedom is directly proportional to the value you can provide to others. Whichever path you choose, your success in life will be directly related to how valuable your skills and contributions are in your chosen field of work. If you are not sure which path to take or what you are doing, focus on getting better at your work. Become more customer focused. Understand what people need. Obtain rare and valuable skills.

Your financial freedom is nobody else's problem and nobody else's business. Why should anyone else care what you want from your life? Why should anyone else help you achieve your goals? People will help you if you help them first. Therefore, if you want to free yourself, improve your skills towards providing a service that is valuable to other people.

Further Resources on Making the Choice

Podcast Episodes

Episode 106—Self-Employed Vs Business Owner[113]

Episode 124—Four Ways To Quit The Rat Race[114]

Episode 125—Q&A on Four Ways To Quit The Rat Race[115]

Episode 218—Choosing A Job-Free Lifestyle[116]

CHAPTER SIX

The Psychological Challenge

One doesn't discover new lands without consenting to lose sight of the shore for a very long time.
—Andre Gide

How Peter's Story Ends

At the beginning of this book, I told you about Peter—the mentor and friend I met as a teenager. Peter had planned to build a business, earn £1 million, and become a successful dropout. His vision for creating a job-free life inspired me to start my own journey of entrepreneurship, and he helped me start my business.

I was following Peter's path. I adopted the same goal: financial independence and a life free of jobs. But our paths diverged.

Over the years, Peter gradually changed. The Sherlock Holmes aspect of his character—his love of ideas—began to disappear. He spoke less about ideas and more about possessions. He began to spend ostentatiously on status symbols. He bought a luxury car and moved into a large house in an exclusive neighborhood. When we first met, we would talk over a curry takeout at his apartment. Later, I would meet him in restaurants, eventually in places where I needed to wear a suit.

Peter became increasingly cynical, especially about relationships. He developed a new preoccupation in life: he wanted to have sex with a lot of beautiful women. He had given up on love. He was not a handsome man, but as he got richer and started to live a more status-oriented lifestyle, he was able to find plenty of beautiful women who wanted to be with him.

I did not know it at the time, but the founding of my business was a turning point in my friendship with Peter. He wanted to take a controlling interest in my business and I did not agree. We worked it out amicably—he lent me the money rather than taking a shareholding—but something had changed, and we were never as close afterwards.

I gradually lost touch with Peter. I was working extremely hard on my business and making less effort to keep in contact, but I also got the sense that he was less inclined to make himself available to meet up. A few years passed when I didn't see him at all.

I finally managed to get Peter to agree to meet with me in 2004, so I could pay back the money that he had lent me to start my business. I was very proud to be able to pay back all the loans with interest because my business was finally making a profit.

I met Peter in a cafe in Little Venice, near his new mansion. He congratulated me on my business and listened with a smile as I told him how things were going. But he had a sad expression in his eyes. He looked tired. I asked how he was doing and what had happened in the years since we last met. What Peter said shocked me.

I learned that Peter had become fabulously rich. He was now a multimillionaire and was continuing to make more money. I also learned that he was deeply unhappy. He had been involved in toxic relationships. He told me a story of betrayal, violence, heartbreak, and isolation. He spoke vaguely of legal conflicts, which I later found out were very serious.

Despite his wealth, Peter worked himself into exhaustion and illness repeatedly. He would push himself incredibly hard for months until he would physically collapse, requiring weeks to recuperate. He had always been intensely focused, but as he got older, his body could not take the pressure of these bursts of activity. He developed health problems.

I got a sense that Peter did not have anyone to talk to. I had always wanted to be closer friends with him, but I never felt able to get close. I don't think anybody could.

I always remembered what Peter had told me a decade earlier about his goal to become a millionaire and retire early. By the time we met in that cafe in 2004, he had long since blown past his £1 million milestone, but he never spoke of his original plans or what he thought of them now. He showed no signs of retiring. Money meant something different to him now. Peter was rich far beyond his original dream, but he had not found fulfillment.

A couple of months after I saw Peter, I invited him to be a guest of honor at a party to celebrate the five-year anniversary of the founding of my business. We presented him with a gift as thanks for having loaned the money that funded the business in the initial stages. He accepted the gift graciously, but never replied to emails after that night. It was the last time I saw him.

I never gave up on Peter's original dream. I always wanted the kind of freedom that Peter had told me about years ago in his little apartment in Greenwich, not the kind of life he eventually chose. Money is a tool for finding freedom. The goal is freedom, not money.

Even though our paths diverged, that conversation with Peter had already changed my life. Peter showed me, by example, that a job-free life is not just possible; it is feasible.

Now that you have read this book, you have had your own version of that life-changing conversation. I had Peter as an example to learn from. You have all the people that I've highlighted in this book. Whereas I learned one path to job freedom (through startup entrepreneurship), you have four different paths to choose from, and I've given you suggestions about how to choose your path.

Three Psychological Challenges

Whichever path to job freedom you choose, you will encounter psychological challenges on your journey. Regardless of which of the four approaches you take, quitting the rat race requires you to find the courage to be unconventional. All four of these lifestyles are unusual ways to live compared to the debt-ridden, day-by-day, jobbing lifestyle that is the norm.

Even though jobs can suck in many ways, they do provide benefits—especially psychological ones. We've focused on how to replace the income you get from a job with income from a job-free life. However, you also need to replace the psychological benefits that a job can give you.

In this final chapter, I provide suggestions on three key psychological challenges for creating a job-free life:

- The challenge of creating a community outside the ready-made community provided by a job.
- The challenge of creating structure in the absence of a job.
- The challenge of finding purpose in your journey.

Community

Jobs provide a ready-made social life. They give you a social network. When you share struggles and achievements with coworkers, it creates a bond. Job-free lifestyles, in contrast, require you to take a more active role in creating a community for yourself.

If you leave your job, you have to be more proactive about nurturing connections with people and creating a community around you. This can be especially difficult, since your job-free lifestyle falls by definition outside the norm.

Friedrich Nietzsche said, "The individual has always had

to struggle to keep from being overwhelmed by the tribe. If you try it, you will be lonely often, and sometimes frightened. But no price is too high to pay for the privilege of owning yourself."

Nietzsche beautifully captured both the pain and the worthiness of determining your life in that quote, but the quote also misses something crucial. We need allies in order to break from the tribe. Although we may like to think of ourselves as self-sufficient individualists, it's vital to cultivate supportive relationships if you want to do something as radical as living free of jobs.

Quitting the rat race to live job free is a life-changing, long-term project. It is incredibly challenging psychologically. Your network of relationships will partly determine whether you can meet that challenge.

I encourage you to find support in your pursuit of a job-free life. You can connect with people online who share your goals. There are good forums for each of the four ways that I have outlined. You can join my Facebook group,[117] and there are also discussion boards on the *Early Retirement Extreme*[118] and *Mr. Money Mustache*[119] websites.

Although creating community for yourself outside a job can be a challenge, it is also an opportunity to find connections that are more authentic. You can devote your energy to connecting with people who inspire you, rather than hanging out with people just because they happen to work in the same place as you. You may lose the default community that comes with your job, but you can build connections with people who share your values.

Personal Relationships

The most important source of social support is your personal relationships. If you have a spouse or partner, their attitude will have a major impact on whether or not you succeed in creating a job-free life.

This person can be your strongest ally in achieving your goal, supporting you both psychologically and practically. A supportive spouse or partner gives you protection against the pressures of conformity.

If you don't have the support of your partner, your journey will be extremely hard. Justin, author of the early-retirement blog *Root of Good*, explains why sharing the same goals as your partner is so crucial to your success:

> One of the biggest impediments to being successful at saving lots of money, growing wealth, and reaching financial independence, is a spouse who is not on board. If you're working on building wealth and the other half of your household is working on spending that wealth, then they can probably spend it faster than you can grow it. You need to be on board with that common goal—whether it is retiring at 40, or even just having a year's worth of cash in the bank in case something happens to one of you (if you lose a job or something). If there is not that common goal in place, then you are working in two different directions and one person is canceling out the other person's hard work.[120]

Creating Structure

Jobs provide structure for your life. They give you a place to go, a set of problems to work on, and a routine to follow.

We need structure in order to get anything done. Getting things done provides the intrinsic motivation of a sense of mastery over your life. When you don't have the structure provided by a job, you have to provide it for yourself.

If you choose an entrepreneurial lifestyle, your level of personal organization can strongly influence your success. I am not naturally talented at task management or project management, but I realized early on in my business that these are crucial skills for entrepreneurs. I invested a lot of effort in learning about how to improve my productivity skills.

The good news is that productivity skills *are* learnable. Even though they don't come naturally to me, I've been able to learn ways to manage tasks and projects effectively. I create structure in my life by relying heavily on productivity *systems*. For example, I use a task management application to organize all my projects and tasks.

My use of productivity systems has been highly influenced by David Allen's approach, known as *Getting Things Done* (GTD).[121] Many other approaches to productivity can also be helpful. The key is not to worry about finding the "best" system, but rather to continually be working on the challenge of productivity. Creating structure for your life is an ongoing process.

Productivity means moving towards your goals, so you can only be productive if you have goals. You can only have goals if you have a sense of purpose. Therefore, in order to be productive, you must identify your purpose in life.

Finding Purpose

If your job does not inspire you, striking out on your own can provide a great opportunity to live a more purposeful life. That was my experience in starting a business. As an entrepreneur, I did the work that was most meaningful to me. Now in writing this book, I am following my purpose of encouraging others to find freedom.

Many people want to quit their jobs, but they don't have a driving sense of purpose. They know that they need to create a source of income to replace their job, but they don't have any mission to guide them.

If you quit a job to pursue any of the job-free lifestyles outlined in this book, you need a strong sense of purpose that can replace the default purpose that you got from your job.

Don't underestimate the importance of this sense of purpose. Even an unfulfilling job can provide some mission, without which life is hard. Jobs give you direction. Outside a job, it is up to you to provide the direction.

Choose a path to job freedom that enables you to find purpose in the *pursuit* of your goal, not just in the outcome. There's no point in trying to be an extreme saver, for example, if you view saving as merely a hassle or an inconvenience. You will only succeed in that route if you find meaning in your journey towards financial independence, including all the lifestyle changes that go with it. The same goes for unjobbing, building a lifestyle business, or building a startup.

All these approaches involve deferring gratification. If

you find purpose in your choice, then you can find joy in the journey too. You can find fulfillment in the pursuit of any of these approaches. You find fulfillment because, by pursuing your goal, you are living your values. That is its own reward.

In the vast, unthinking universe, we are so lucky to have consciousness. We have the choice of what to make of our lives. We can choose to free ourselves from jobs. We owe it to ourselves to take advantage of the amazing opportunity.

It is easy to imagine that you will find a time in the future to do epic things. But your time is going to run out. The fact that we are all going to die is a wonderful motivation to get on with living life to the fullest while we can. The pursuit of a job-free life will enable you to live your highest purpose.

Appendix: About Investing

Investing should be more like watching paint dry or watching grass grow. If you want excitement, take $800 and go to Las Vegas.
—Paul Samuelson

This appendix provides an overview of the practical issues involved in investing and living from investments. These issues are especially relevant if you aim to achieve financial independence, for example through extreme saving or selling a startup. However, they are also relevant for everyone interested in increasing their financial freedom.

There are three key topics that you will need to consider:

- Choosing your approach to investing
- Deciding on a portfolio design
- Working out how you can live sustainably from your investments (e.g., how much money you need to accumulate, and how much you think you can spend each year).

This is an introduction, providing only an overview of these topics. I provide resources for further reading at the end.

Choosing Your Approach to Investing

The first step in deciding how to invest your money is to decide on your overall approach to investing. In particular, there are two distinctive approaches—active investing and passive investing—which arise from different assumptions and lead to different strategies.

The active investing approach assumes that it is possible to predict investment price movements in advance, using superior insights. Active investors aim to earn above average returns, based on predictions that are more accurate than those of the majority of market participants. They purchase and sell securities depending on their predictions of upcoming changes in market conditions. Some active investors make predictions themselves. Others place their trust in a professional investor to do so on their behalf.

In contrast, the passive investing approach does not attempt to predict price movements. Instead, passive investors create a "set it and forget it" strategy that they stick to, regardless of what happens to the market. Passive investors believe that it is easier to make money by identifying a simple strategy and sticking to it, than by trying to predict trends. They believe that there is so much unpredictability in markets that speculators will be frequently wrong-footed. For these reasons, they believe that a fixed strategy will accumulate more over time. Passive investors often emphasize that the evidence favors their approach, since passive investment funds have demonstrated better performance over time than active ones.[122]

A passive investment strategy prevents you from overreacting to the latest scares or hot tips and keeps your emotion out of the investment decisions. When I interviewed Mike from *Mike and Lauren*[123], he described the psychological rationale for his approach to passive investing using index funds:

> Your biggest enemy in investing is yourself, because we are programmed to buy high and sell low. It is an emotional game more than a mathematical game. Mathematical studies have shown that it is fairly difficult to beat the market average and that index investing is, if not the best way, one of the best and simplest ways there are to increase your wealth. So it's a game you play with yourself—just not checking the prices every day and, when it goes down, not paying attention to it.[124]

I have chosen to use a passive investment strategy for the vast majority of my money. I've done this for two reasons. Firstly, the evidence convinces me that passive investments perform better over time, compared to active strategies.

Secondly, when I quit the rat race, I did not want to take on a new job of being a full-time investor. It would have defeated the objective of achieving financial independence for me if I then ended up fussing over my portfolio all day long, wondering whether I should be buying or selling. I didn't want to get to early retirement just to find I have a new job as a portfolio manager. Instead, I wanted the freedom to do creative things with my time and not to spend all my time managing my money.

Investing can take up your entire life if you want it to. It can certainly become your new job once you retire. Whatever your view on the merits of speculating, I think it is prudent to adopt a passive, long-term strategy for the majority of your investments. Not only does the evidence suggest that passive investing is the better strategy overall, but there is also a lot more to life than managing your money. Speculate with a little for fun if you want to, but give yourself time to enjoy your freedom. The greatest benefit of financial freedom is that it gives you time to do whatever you want with your life.

Designing a Portfolio

If you adopt a passive investing approach, you still need to decide on a specific portfolio design. This means choosing the asset classes you want to hold in your portfolio, the quantities of each asset class, and the rebalancing rules that you will use for the portfolio going forward. Furthermore, you must decide on the details of which individual securities you will purchase, within each asset class.

Portfolio design is a huge topic, which I can only introduce here. There are many considerations that will be specific to your unique circumstances—your location, your tax liabilities, and your own approach to investing. There are no short cuts—you simply need to spend the time learning about investing and, most importantly, getting good advice.

A great resource to start learning about different passive investment portfolios is the website *Portfolio Charts*.[125] On this website, you can see a range of passive portfolio designs and test different asset allocations against historical data from US markets. This gives you a sense of the pros and cons of different portfolios. You can hear my interview with Tyler, the creator of this site, in episode 223 of my podcast.[126]

Many passive investors use the approach outlined by

John Bogle, a pioneer of low-cost index funds and author of *The Little Book of Common Sense Investing*.[127] Those following his approach tend to hold a portfolio consisting mainly of an index fund of stocks, with some smaller proportion held in an index fund of bonds. Typically, these investors undertake periodic rebalancing of their portfolios to maintain the ratio of stocks to bonds within a certain range.

I use a passive investment approach known as the Permanent Portfolio. The original developer of this approach was the libertarian author and investment advisor, Harry Browne. The Permanent Portfolio strategy is to hold fixed investments in four different asset classes with periodic rebalancing. The four asset classes are stocks, long-term bonds, gold, and cash. The idea is to hold these assets long term and rebalance all of them back to 25 percent whenever one asset class goes above or below a certain rebalancing band. This strategy is designed to give lower volatility, while still providing adequate returns.

Living from Investments

There are two questions facing you if you want to live from your investments:
- How much money will you need to save first?
- Once you have saved enough, how much money can you sustainably withdraw from your portfolio each year?

There is a lot of debate about how much you can expect to withdraw sustainably from a portfolio.[128] To cut a long story short, the figure that has the most consensus for a *sustainable withdrawal rate* is four percent of your capital,[129] for typical passive investment portfolios. In other words, many people who have researched safe withdrawal rates using historical data have estimated that you could probably spend the cash equivalent of four percent of your total investment portfolio each year. If you invest wisely, your portfolio is likely to earn enough to cover inflation and the four percent that you are spending. The idea of financial independence is to live from a sustainable withdrawal rate without eating into your capital to the extent that you will run out of money.

The four percent annual withdrawal rate implies that your accumulation target (the amount you need to save for financial independence) is 25 times your annual living expenses. On a monthly basis, your accumulation target amount is 300 times your monthly living expenses (25*12). Many people use this relationship between their expenses and the four percent rule to estimate how much money they need to save in order to reach financial independence.

Of course, there are no guarantees that your portfolio will generate enough of a return to cover a safe four percent drawdown once you have quit the rat race. Even if you follow a sensible investment strategy, in some years you will probably earn less or even take a loss, owing to market volatility. If you experience many bad years very early on in your retirement, the impact on your portfolio will be much worse than if you experience them later.[130]

The four percent rule is uncertain. Past returns are the

most useful data we have to test the sustainability of different portfolio allocations and withdrawal rates. The four percent rule would have been sustainable for a simple stock and bond portfolio in the majority of years of retirement for which we have data (but not all of them). But, as you have no doubt heard many times, past returns do not guarantee future success.

This uncertainty does not stop those who aim for financial independence as part of a job-free lifestyle. It's true that there is no guarantee that you won't run out of money, but you can develop a plan B for what to do if your portfolio were to go badly. There is no rule that says you have to sit on your hands if your financial situation is less sustainable than you thought.

Some early retirees take a "just in case" approach and choose to live even more frugally than the four percent rule suggests. They withdraw three percent of their portfolios instead, leaving some leeway in case they have lower than expected investment returns. The lower withdrawal rate allows their portfolios to compound more in good years, making it even safer.

Others choose to combine the unjobbing approach and earn a little money on the side from a project they love doing. They supplement their investment income so that they can take less than four percent from the portfolio.

The worst-case scenario is that you might deplete your portfolio to the point that you have to go back to work. In such a case, you might not be able to earn as much as you did the last time you had a job, especially if you have been out of employment for some time. This worst-case scenario did not discourage me. I considered it a risk worth taking for the freedom that living a job-free life gives me.

Further Resources on Investing

Podcast Episodes

Episode 49—Financial Preparedness: An Interview with Medium Tex[131]

Episode 76—The Permanent Portfolio: Author Interview with Craig Rowland[132]

Episode 167—Radical Personal Finance Interview: The Permanent Portfolio[133]

Episode 223—A Guide to Passive Investment Portfolios: Interview With Tyler from Portfolio Charts[134]

Books

John Bogle's book, *The Little Book of Common Sense Investing*[135], is a useful introduction to the concept of passive investing, with a focus on stocks and bonds. Burton Malkiel's book, *A Random Walk Down Wall Street*,[136] provides a more academic explanation of why passive investment funds tend to outperform active funds.

If you are interested in the Permanent Portfolio, you can read Harry Browne's own summary of his approach in his book, *Fail-Safe Investing.*[137] A more detailed explanation can be found in a book by Craig Rowland and Mike Lawson called *The Permanent Portfolio*[138].

For a discussion of the technical issues related to living from investments, see Todd Tresidder's book, *The 4% Rule and Safe Withdrawal Rates in Retirement.*[139]

Websites

The best resource for reviewing passive investment portfolios is the *Portfolio Charts*[140] website. This is a great resource to start with to compare different portfolio designs.

Josh Kaufman, author of *The Personal MBA*, has written a good introductory post about the Permanent Portfolio strategy on his blog.[141] Craig Rowland's Permanent Portfolio discussion forum[142] is a great source of information on this strategy.

For websites related to living from investments, Wade Pfau has very detailed technical articles at his *Retirement Researcher* website.[143] Mr. Money Mustache provides lots of useful material at his website, especially in the article "The Shockingly Simple Math Behind Early Retirement."[144]

Bibliography

Allen, David. *Getting Things Done: The Art of Stress-Free Productivity*. New York: Penguin Books, 2001.

Allen, David. *Making It All Work: Winning at the Game of Work and the Business of Life*. New York: Penguin Books, 2009.

Bogle, John. *The Little Book of Common Sense Investing: The Only Way to Guarantee Your Fair Share of Market Returns*. Hoboken, N.J.: John Wiley & Sons, 2007.

Browne, Harry. *Fail-Safe Investing: Lifelong Financial Safety in 30 Minutes*. New York: St. Martin's Press, 1999.

Browne, Harry. *How I Found Freedom in an Unfree World: A Handbook for Personal Liberty*. 25th Anniv. ed. Great Falls, Mont.: LiamWorks, 1998.

Burlingham, Bo. *Finish Big: How Great Entrepreneurs Exit Their Companies on Top*. New York: Portfolio Penguin, 2014.

Dacyczyn, Amy. *The Tightwad Gazette: Big Money-Saving Guide*. 2002 ed. New York: Gramercy Books, 2002.

Desyllas, Jake. *Becoming an Entrepreneur: How to Find Freedom and Fulfillment as a Business Owner*. London: Amazon, 2014.

Dominguez, Joseph R., and Vicki Robin. *Your Money or Your Life: Transforming Your Relationship with Money and Achieving Financial Independence,* rev. ed. London: Penguin, 2008.

Ferriss, Timothy. *The 4-Hour Workweek: Escape 9—5, Live Anywhere, and Join the New Rich.* New York: Crown Publishers, 2007.

Fisker, Jacob Lund. *Early Retirement Extreme: A Philosophical And Practical Guide To Financial Independence.* United States: CreateSpace, 2010.

Flynn, Pat. *Let Go.* Amazon, 2013.

Fogler, Michael. *Un-Jobbing: The Adult Liberation Handbook*, 2nd ed. Lexington, Ky.: Free Choice Press, 1999.

French, Douglas E. *Walk Away: The Rise and Fall of the Home-Ownership Myth.* Auburn, AL: Ludwig von Mises Institute, 2010.

Fried, Jason and David Heinemeier Hansson, *Rework.* New York: Random House 2010.

Gerber, Michael E. *The E-myth Revisited: Why Most Small Businesses Don't Work and What to Do About It.* New York: HarperCollins, 1995.

Kawasaki, Guy. *The Art of the Start: The Time-Tested, Battle-Hardened Guide for Anyone Starting Anything.* New York: Portfolio, 2004.

Kirkpatrick, Darrow. *Retiring Sooner: How to Accelerate Your Financial Independence.* Amazon, 2013.

Malkiel, Burton Gordon. *A Random Walk Down Wall Street: The Time-Tested Strategy for Successful Investing.* New York: W.W. Norton, 2003.

Mises, Ludwig von. *Socialism: An Economic and Sociological Analysis.* New ed. New Haven: Yale University Press, 1951.

Pierce, Linda Breen. *Choosing Simplicity: Real People Finding Peace and Fulfillment in a Complex World.* Carmel, CA: Gallagher Press, 2000.

Ries, Eric. *The Lean Startup: How Today's Entrepreneurs Use Continuous Innovation to Create Radically Successful Businesses.* New York: Crown Business, 2011.

Rothbard, Murray. *What Has Government Done to Our Money?* Auburn, AL: Ludwig von Mises Institute, 1990.

Rowland, Craig, and Mike Lawson. *The Permanent Portfolio: Harry Browne's Long-Term Investment Strategy.* Hoboken, N.J.: Wiley, 2012.

Silverstein, Michael J., and Neil Fiske. *Trading Up: Why Consumers Want New Luxury Goods and How Companies Create Them.* New York: Portfolio, 2003.

Sivers, Derek. *Anything You Want.* Amazon, 2011.

Stanley, Thomas J. *Stop Acting Rich: ... and Start Living like a Real Millionaire.* Hoboken, N.J.: Wiley, 2009.

Stanley, Thomas J., and William D. Danko. *The Millionaire Next Door: The Surprising Secrets of America's Wealthy.* Atlanta, Ga.: Longstreet Press, 1996.

Terhorst, Paul. *Cashing in on the American Dream: How to Retire at 35.* Toronto: Bantam Books, 1988.

Thomas, Chris. *You Have Too Much Shit.* Published online at http://youhavetoomuchshit.com/

Tresidder, Todd. *The 4% Rule and Safe Withdrawal Rates In Retirement (60 Minute Financial Solutions).*

Amazon, 2012.

Todd R. Tresidder, *How Much Money Do I Need to Retire? (60 Minute Financial Solutions)* Amazon, 2012.

Walsh, Peter. *It's All Too Much: An Easy Plan for Living a Richer Life with Less Stuff.* New York: Free Press, 2007.

Warrillow, John. *Built to Sell: Creating a Business That Can Thrive Without You.* New York: Portfolio Hardcover, 2011.

Acknowledgements

I am grateful to all the people who helped me create this book. Special thanks to Hannah Braime and Matt Amberson for all their feedback and support. Thanks so much to my beta readers: Alan Lynch, Andrew Barlament, Andy Norris, Benjamin Roth, Cameron Harris, Chris H., Dale Patterson, Daniel Lothrop, Daniel Mackler, David Albrecht, David Downie, David Stanek, Dirk Fritze, Dom Mozel, Ed Salamanca, Emily Crotteau, Ernest L. Ortiz, Frank Thomas-Hockey, Gretchen Clark, Guiselle Ashton, Hannah Thomson, Ian, Ian Thompson, Ib Vegger, Indrė Urbonaitė, James Piers Taylor, James Walpole, Jason L. Hendren, Jason R., Jenna VanLeeuwen, Jeremy Strozer, Jim Mitchell, Justin Cullinane, Katie, Kayla Mae Anderson, Laura Reichardt, Luis G. Peña, Marc Hoffmann, Martin Hamilton, Martin Ronckevic, Mary Bright, Matt H., Michael Day, Michael January, Nathaniel Graham, Nick Archer, Nick Edmonds, Nick Sarris, Nicklas W. Bjurman, Pablo Pérez, Paul VandenBosch, Peter Glink, Rien van der Lugt, Rob Litzke, Robert Snyder, Robert van der H., Russell Graves, Ryan, Sarah Burch, Shahrukh N. Bakar, Steve Franssen, Steve Reed, Steve Wellings, Terry Brock,

Thomas Bell, Tobias Locsei, Wendi Pilling, Wolfgang Muenst, and Zsolt Babocsai.

About the Author

Jake Desyllas is an investor and author who writes about entrepreneurship, financial independence, and freedom. In 2000, he founded *Intelligent Space*, an award-winning consultancy that led innovation in the field of pedestrian movement simulation and analysis. In 2010, he sold his business, quit the rat race, and retired early at the age of thirty-eight. He is the author of *Becoming an Entrepreneur: How To Find Freedom and Fulfillment as a Business Owner*. He is the host of a podcast called *The Voluntary Life*.

He has a bachelors degree, a masters degree, and a doctorate. He is a perpetual traveler, a minimalist, a productivity-systems enthusiast, an avid reader of philosophy and psychology, and a marathon inline skater.

Endnotes

[1] Jake Desyllas, *Becoming an Entrepreneur: How to Find Freedom and Fulfillment as a Business Owner*. Voluntary Life Press, 2014.

[2] http://www.thevoluntarylife.com

[3] Joseph R. Dominguez and Vicki Robin, *Your Money or Your Life: Transforming Your Relationship with Money and Achieving Financial Independence*, rev. ed. London: Penguin, 2008.

[4] *Root of Good,* http://rootofgood.com

[5] *Go Curry Cracker,* http://www.gocurrycracker.com

[6] *Early Retirement Extreme,* http://earlyretirementextreme.com

[7] Jacob Lund Fisker, *Early Retirement Extreme: A Philosophical and Practical Guide to Financial Independence*. United States: CreateSpace Independent Publishing Platform, 2010

[8] Amy Dacyczyn, *The Tightwad Gazette: Big Money-Saving Guide*. New York: Gramercy Books, 2002.

[9] Data cited in Dominguez and Robin, *Your Money or Your Life.*

[10] *Mr. Money Mustache,* http://www.mrmoneymustache.com

[11] *Mike and Lauren,* http://www.mikeandlauren.com

[12] *Mike and Lauren TV,* http://www.youtube.com/user/MikeAndLaurenTV

[13] *The Voluntary Life,* podcast episode 164, "We Plan to Retire at 30: Interview with Mike and Lauren" http://www.thevoluntarylife.com/2014/07/164-we-plan-to-retire-at-30-interview.html

[14] For a more detailed discussion of these numbers, see Mr. Money Mustache's article, "T*he Shockingly Simple Math Behind Early Retirement"* at http://www.mrmoneymustache.com/2012/01/13/the-shockingly-simple-math-behind-early-retirement/

[15] *The Voluntary Life,* Episode 162, "Spend Little, Save More, Travel the World: Interview with Go Curry Cracker," http://www.thevoluntarylife.com/2014/07/162-spend-little-save-more-travel-world.html

[16] Thomas J. Stanley and William D. Danko, *The Millionaire Next Door: The Surprising Secrets of America's Wealthy.* Atlanta, Ga.: Longstreet Press, 1996.

[17] Thomas J. Stanley, Ph.D. blog, "Building Wealth Revisited," November 4, 2014, http://www.thomasjstanley.com/blog-articles/596/Building_Wealth_Revisited.html

[18] *The Voluntary Life*, episode 166, "Retired at 33: Interview with Justin from Root of Good," http://www.thevoluntarylife.com/2014/07/166-retired-at-33-interview-with-justin.html

[19] *The Voluntary Life,* Episode 164, "We Plan To Retire At

30: Interview with Mike and Lauren," http://www.thevoluntarylife.com/2014/07/164-we-plan-to-retire-at-30-interview.html

[20] *The Voluntary Life,* Episode 162

[21] The Voluntary Life Podcast Episode 162—Spend Little, Save More, Travel the World: Interview with Go Curry Cracker http://www.thevoluntarylife.com/2014/07/162-spend-little-save-more-travel-world.html

[22] The Voluntary Life Podcast Episode 162—Spend Little, Save More, Travel the World: Interview with Go Curry Cracker http://www.thevoluntarylife.com/2014/07/162-spend-little-save-more-travel-world.html

[23] Michael J. Silverstein and Neil Fiske, *Trading Up: Why Consumers Want New Luxury Goods and How Companies Create Them.* New York: Portfolio, 2003.

[24] The Voluntary Life Podcast Episode 162—Spend Little, Save More, Travel the World: Interview with Go Curry Cracker http://www.thevoluntarylife.com/2014/07/162-spend-little-save-more-travel-world.html

[25] in the UK, this is referred to as the Annual Allowance (AA).

[26] In the UK, this is referred to as the Lifetime Allowance (LTA).

[27] From The Money Advice Service:

"The Lifetime Allowance for most people is £1.25 million in the tax year 2014—15 (reduced from £1.5 million in 2013—14)."

https://www.moneyadviceservice.org.uk/en/articles/the-lifetime-allowance-for-pension-savings

[28] *Radical Personal Finance,* http://radicalpersonalfinance.com

[29] More discussion of this technique can be found in *The Voluntary Life*, episode 209, "Tax Strategies and Financial Freedom, Part 1 (Interview With Joshua Sheats)," http://www.thevoluntarylife.com/2015/06/209-tax-strategies-and-financial.html.

[30] Dr. Ros Altmann blog, "Polish pension confiscation — a threat to funded private pensions or a one-off?" http://pensionsandsavings.com/pensions/polish-pension-confiscation-how-can-we-protect-private-pensions/

[31] ibid

[32] Carlos Alberto Quiroga, "Bolivia Moves to Nationalize Pensions," Reuters, November 16, 2010, http://www.reuters.com/article/2010/11/16/us-bolivia-pensions-idUSTRE6AF5Z120101116

[33] Allison Schrager, "Unlike Russia, the US Government Won't Take Your Pension Outright," August 18, 2014, http://www.businessweek.com/articles/2014-08-18/russia-seized-citizens-pension-funds-dot-could-that-happen-in-the-u-dot-s-dot

[34] http://www.thevoluntarylife.com/2014/07/162-spend-little-save-more-travel-world.html

[35] http://www.thevoluntarylife.com/2014/07/164-we-plan-to-retire-at-30-interview.html

[36] http://www.thevoluntarylife.com/2014/07/166-retired-at-33-interview-with-justin.html

[37] http://www.thevoluntarylife.com/2015/06/209-tax-strategies-and-financial.html

[38] Dominguez, Joseph R., and Vicki Robin. *Your Money Or Your Life: Transforming Your Relationship With Money And Achieving Financial Independence*. London: Penguin, 2008 (revised edition).

[39] Fisker, Jacob Lund. *Early Retirement Extreme: A Philosophical And Practical Guide To Financial Independence*. United States: [s.n.], 2010.

[40] Paul Terhorst, *Cashing In on the American Dream: How to Retire at 35*. Toronto: Bantam Books, 1988.

[41] Michael Fogler, *Un-Jobbing: The Adult Liberation Handbook*. 2nd ed. Lexington, Ky.: Free Choice Press, 1999.

[42] *The Voluntary Life,* podcast episode 34, "Unjobbing: Author Interview with Michael Fogler," http://www.thevoluntarylife.com/2011/12/unjobbing-author-interview-with-michael.html

[43] Fogler, *Un-jobbing,* page 10

[44] Linda Breen Pierce, *Choosing Simplicity: Real People Finding Peace and Fulfillment in a Complex World*. Carmel, CA: Gallagher Press, 2000.

[45] Elliot Hulse, *Elliot Said What,* http://www.youtube.com/user/elliottsaidwhat

[46] Elliot Hulse, *NonJobs: Turn Your Passion Into Profits,* http://nonjob.com

[47] *The Voluntary Life,* podcast episode 128, "Be More Expansive Than Your Expertise: An Interview With Elliott Hulse," http://www.thevoluntarylife.com/2013/10/128-be-more-expansive-than-your.html

[48] Fogler, *Un-Jobbing,* page 15

[49] *The Voluntary Life*, episode 128

[50] The Voluntary Life Podcast Episode 118—Decluttering And Community Selling: Interview with Jorja Leavitt http://www.thevoluntarylife.com/2013/07/118-decluttering-and-community-selling.html

[51] Douglas E. French, *Walk Away: The Rise and Fall of the Home-Ownership Myth.* Auburn, AL: Ludwig von Mises Institute, 2010.

[52] *Post-Consumer Life* http://postconsumerlife.com

[53] *The Voluntary Life,* podcast episode 171, "From Million Dollar House To Tiny Home: Interview with Jacki Rigoni," http://www.thevoluntarylife.com/2014/09/171-from-million-dollar-house-to-tiny.html

[54] Ludwig von Mises, *Socialism: An Economic and Sociological Analysis.* New ed. New Haven: Yale University Press, 1951.

[55] *The Voluntary Life,* Episode 34

[56] Fogler, *Un-Jobbing,* page 71

[57] http://www.thevoluntarylife.com/2011/12/unjobbing-author-interview-with-michael.html

[58] http://www.thevoluntarylife.com/2013/07/118-decluttering-and-community-selling.html

[59] http://www.thevoluntarylife.com/2013/10/128-be-more-expansive-than-your.html

[60] http://www.thevoluntarylife.com/2014/09/171-from-million-dollar-house-to-tiny.html

[61] Fogler, Michael. <u>Un-Jobbing: The Adult Liberation Handbook.</u> 2nd ed. Lexington, Ky.: Free Choice Press, 1999.

[62] Walsh, Peter. *It's All Too Much: An Easy Plan For Living A Richer Life With Less Stuff.* New York: Free Press, 2007.

[63] http://youhavetoomuchshit.com/download/You_Have_-Too_Much_Shit.pdf

[64] *Smart Passive Income,* http://www.smartpassiveincome.com

[65] Pat Flynn, *Let Go.* Amazon, 2013.

[66] Timothy Ferriss, *The 4-Hour Workweek: Escape 9—5, Live Anywhere, and Join the New Rich.* New York: Crown Publishers, 2007.

[67] Out Of The Box, http://www.outoftheboxpodcast.com

[68] *The Voluntary Life,* podcast episode 147, "Out Of The Box Interview: Financial Freedom and Personal Development" http://www.thevoluntarylife.com/2014/03/147-out-of-box-interview-financial.html

[69] *Financial Mentor,* http://financialmentor.com

[70] Todd R. Tresidder, *How Much Money Do I Need to Retire?* Amazon, 2012.

[71] *The Voluntary Life,* podcast episode 119, "How To Develop Your Wealth Plan: An Interview With Todd Tressider" http://www.thevoluntarylife.com/2013/07/119-how-to-develop-your-wealth-plan.html

[72] The Voluntary Life Podcast Episode 131— Perpetual Travellers Part 3: Interview with David Kahn http://www.thevoluntarylife.com/2013/10/131-perpetual-travellers-part-3.html

[73] Radical Personal Finance, http://radicalpersonalfinance.com

[74] *The Voluntary Life,* podcast episode 209 "Tax Strategies and Financial Freedom Part 1 (Interview with Joshua Sheats)" http://www.thevoluntarylife.com/2015/06/209-

tax-strategies-and-financial.html

[75] *The Voluntary Life,* podcast episode 119, "How to Develop Your Wealth Plan: An Interview with Todd Tressider" http://www.thevoluntarylife.com/2013/07/119-how-to-develop-your-wealth-plan.html

[76] *The Voluntary Life,* podcast episode 130, "Perpetual Travellers Part 2: Interview With Pete Sisco" http://www.thevoluntarylife.com/2013/10/130-perpetual-travellers-part-2.html

[77] *The Voluntary Life,* podcast episode 131 "Perpetual Travellers Part 3: Interview with David Kahn" http://www.thevoluntarylife.com/2013/10/131-perpetual-travellers-part-3.html

[78] *The Voluntary Life,* podcast episode 130 "Perpetual Travellers Part 2: Interview With Pete Sisco" http://www.thevoluntarylife.com/2013/10/130-perpetual-travellers-part-2.html

[79] See my book, *Becoming An Entrepreneur,* for a discussion of finding purpose in business.

[80] http://www.thevoluntarylife.com/2013/07/119-how-to-develop-your-wealth-plan.html

[81] http://www.thevoluntarylife.com/2013/10/130-perpetual-travellers-part-2.html

[82] http://www.thevoluntarylife.com/2013/10/131-perpetual-travellers-part-3.html

[83] http://www.thevoluntarylife.com/2014/03/147-out-of-box-interview-financial.html

[84] http://www.thevoluntarylife.com/2015/06/209-tax-strategies-and-financial.html

[85] Timothy Ferriss, *The 4-Hour Workweek: Escape 9-5, Live Anywhere, And Join The New Rich*. New York: Crown Publishers, 2007.

[86] Pat Flynn, *Let Go*. Amazon, 2013

[87] Michael E. Gerber, *The E-myth Revisited: Why Most Small Businesses Don't Work and What to Do About It*. New York: HarperCollins, 1995.

[88] Jason Fried and David Heinemeier Hansson, *Rework*. New York: Random House 2010

[89] Harry Browne, *How I Found Freedom in an Unfree World: A Handbook for Personal Liberty*. 25th Anniv. ed. Great Falls, Mont.: LiamWorks, 1998.

[90] Jake Desyllas, *Becoming An Entrepreneur: How To Find Freedom And Fulfillment As A Business Owner*. London: Amazon, 2014

[91] CD Baby Inc., http://www.cdbaby.com/

[92] Derek Sivers, *Anything You Want*. Amazon, 2011.

[93] Jason Fried and David Heinemeier Hansson make this case in their excellent book, *Rework* (Random House, 2010). They argue that creating a business only makes sense if you love it so much that you want to continue doing it indefinitely. They believe it is is self-defeating to treat a business as a means to a final cash out because you risk spending a lot of time and effort chasing a goal without getting fulfillment from doing the work itself, which does not lead to great work.

[94] John Warrillow, *Built to sell: Creating a Business That Can Thrive Without You*. New York: Portfolio Hardcover, 2011.

[95] Gerber, Michael E. *The E-myth Revisited: Why Most Small Businesses Don't Work and What to Do About It*. New York: HarperCollins, 1995.

[96] Jake Desyllas, *Becoming An Entrepreneur: How To Find Freedom And Fulfilment As A Business Owner*. London: Amazon, 2014

[97] John Warrillow, "3 Things That Happen When You Make a Million Dollars," Inc.com, October 27, 2014, http://www.inc.com/john-warrillow/3-things-that-happen-when-you-make-a-million-dollars.html.

[98] The valuation is usually based on some multiple of earnings before interest, taxes, and amortization (EBITA). More discussion about valuation can be found in: Bo Burlingham, *Finish Big: How Great Entrepreneurs Exit Their Companies on Top*. New York: Portfolio Penguin, 2014.

[99] http://www.thevoluntarylife.com/2012/05/entrepreneurship-part-8-selling-your.html

[100] http://www.thevoluntarylife.com/2013/05/107-what-kind-of-business-should-i-start.html

[101] http://www.thevoluntarylife.com/2013/08/121-big-decisions-for-entrepreneurs.html

[102] http://www.thevoluntarylife.com/2014/06/161-review-of-built-to-sell-by-john.html

[103] http://www.thevoluntarylife.com/2015/06/207-who-will-buy-your-business.html

[104] Jake Desyllas, Becoming An Entrepreneur: How To Find Freedom And Fulfillment As A Business Owner. London: Amazon, 2014

[105] Eric Ries, *The Lean Startup: How Today's Entrepreneurs Use Continuous Innovation to Create Radically Successful Businesses.* New York: Crown Business, 2011.

[106] Guy Kawasaki, *The Art of the Start: The Time-Tested, Battle-Hardened Guide for Anyone Starting Anything.* New York: Portfolio, 2004.

[107] Derek Sivers, *Anything You Want.* Amazon, 2011.

[108] John Warrillow, *Built To Sell: Creating A Business That Can Thrive Without You.* New York: Portfolio Hardcover, 2011.

[109] Bo Burlingham, *Finish Big: How Great Entrepreneurs Exit Their Companies on Top.* New York: Portfolio Penguin, 2014.

[110] Michael E. Gerber, *The E-myth Revisited: Why Most Small Businesses Don't Work and What to Do About It.* New York: HarperCollins, 1995.

[111] Jason Fried and David Heinemeier Hansson, *Rework.* New York: Random House 2010

[112] Harry Browne, *How I Found Freedom in an Unfree World: A Handbook for Personal Liberty.* 25th Anniv. ed. Great Falls, Mont.: LiamWorks, 1998.

[113] http://www.thevoluntarylife.com/2013/05/106-self-employed-vs-business-owner.html

[114] http://www.thevoluntarylife.com/2013/09/124-four-ways-to-quit-rat-race.html

[115] http://www.thevoluntarylife.com/2013/09/125-q-on-four-ways-to-quit-rat-race.html

[116] http://www.thevoluntarylife.com/2015/08/218-choosing-job-free-lifestyle.html

[117] The Voluntary Life Community, https://www.facebook.com/groups/TheVoluntaryLifeCommunity/

[118] http://earlyretirementextreme.com

[119] http://www.mrmoneymustache.com

[120] *The Voluntary Life,* podcast episode 166, "Retired at 33: Interview with Justin from Root of Good" http://www.thevoluntarylife.com/2014/07/166-retired-at-33-interview-with-justin.html

[121] David Allen, *Getting Things Done: The Art of Stress-Free Productivity.* New York: Penguin Books, 2001.

[122] The evidence for the better longer term performance of passive investment is summarised in Burton Gordon Malkiel, *A Random Walk Down Wall Street: the Time-Tested Strategy for Successful Investing.* New York: W.W. Norton, 2003.

[123] http://www.youtube.com/user/MikeAndLaurenTV

[124] *The Voluntary Life,* episode 164, "We Plan To Retire At 30: Interview with Mike and Lauren" http://www.thevoluntarylife.com/2014/07/164-we-plan-to-retire-at-30-interview.html

[125] *Portfolio Charts,* http://portfoliocharts.com

[126] *The Voluntary Life,* podcast episode 223, "A Guide to Passive Investment Portfolios: Interview with Tyler from Portfolio Charts" http://www.thevoluntarylife.com/2015/10/223-guide-to-passive-investment.html

[127] John Bogle, *The Little Book of Common Sense Investing: The Only Way to Guarantee Your Fair Share of Market Returns.* Hoboken, N.J.: John Wiley & Sons, 2007.

[128] You can find an extensive discussion of the four percent

rule and it's limitations in Tresidder, *The 4% Rule and Safe Withdrawal Rates In Retirement (60 Minute Financial Solutions)*. Amazon 2012.

[129] Mr. Money Mustache provides a good explanation of the four percent rule in the article, "The Shockingly Simple Math Behind Early Retirement," Mr. Money Mustache blog, January 13, 2012, http://www.mrmoneymustache.com/2012/01/13/the-shockingly-simple-math-behind-early-retirement/

[130] This is called sequence-of-returns risk.

[131] http://www.thevoluntarylife.com/2012/04/financial-preparedness-interview-with.html

[132] http://www.thevoluntarylife.com/2012/09/76-permanent-portfolio-author-interview.html

[133] http://www.thevoluntarylife.com/2014/08/167-radical-personal-finance-interview.html

[134] http://www.thevoluntarylife.com/2015/10/223-guide-to-passive-investment.html

[135] Bogle, John. *The Little Book of Common Sense Investing: the Only Way to Guarantee Your Fair Share of Market Returns.* Hoboken, N.J.: John Wiley & Sons, 2007. Print.

[136] Burton Gordon Malkiel, *A Random Walk Down Wall Street: the Time-Tested Strategy for Successful Investing.* [Completely rev. and updated]. ed. New York: W.W. Norton, 2003.

[137] Harry Browne, *Fail-safe investing: lifelong financial safety in 30 minutes.* New York: St. Martin's Press, 1999.

[138] Craig Rowland and Mike Lawson. *The permanent portfolio: Harry Browne's long-term investment strategy.* Hobo-

ken, N.J.: Wiley, 2012.

[139] Todd Tresidder, *The 4% Rule and Safe Withdrawal Rates In Retirement (60 Minute Financial Solutions)*. Amazon 2012.

[140] *Portfolio Charts,* http://portfoliocharts.com

[141] Josh Kaufman blog, "Permanent Portfolio Investing Strategy," https://joshkaufman.net/permanent-portfolio/

[142] Permanent Portfolio Discussion Forum, http://www.gyroscopicinvesting.com/forum/

[143] *Retirement Researcher,* http://retirementresearcher.com

[144] http://www.mrmoneymustache.com/2012/01/13/the-shockingly-simple-math-behind-early-retirement/

Printed in Great Britain
by Amazon